Infamous Cults: The Life and Crimes of Cult Leaders and Their Followers

Infamous Crimes, Volume 1

Daniela Airlie

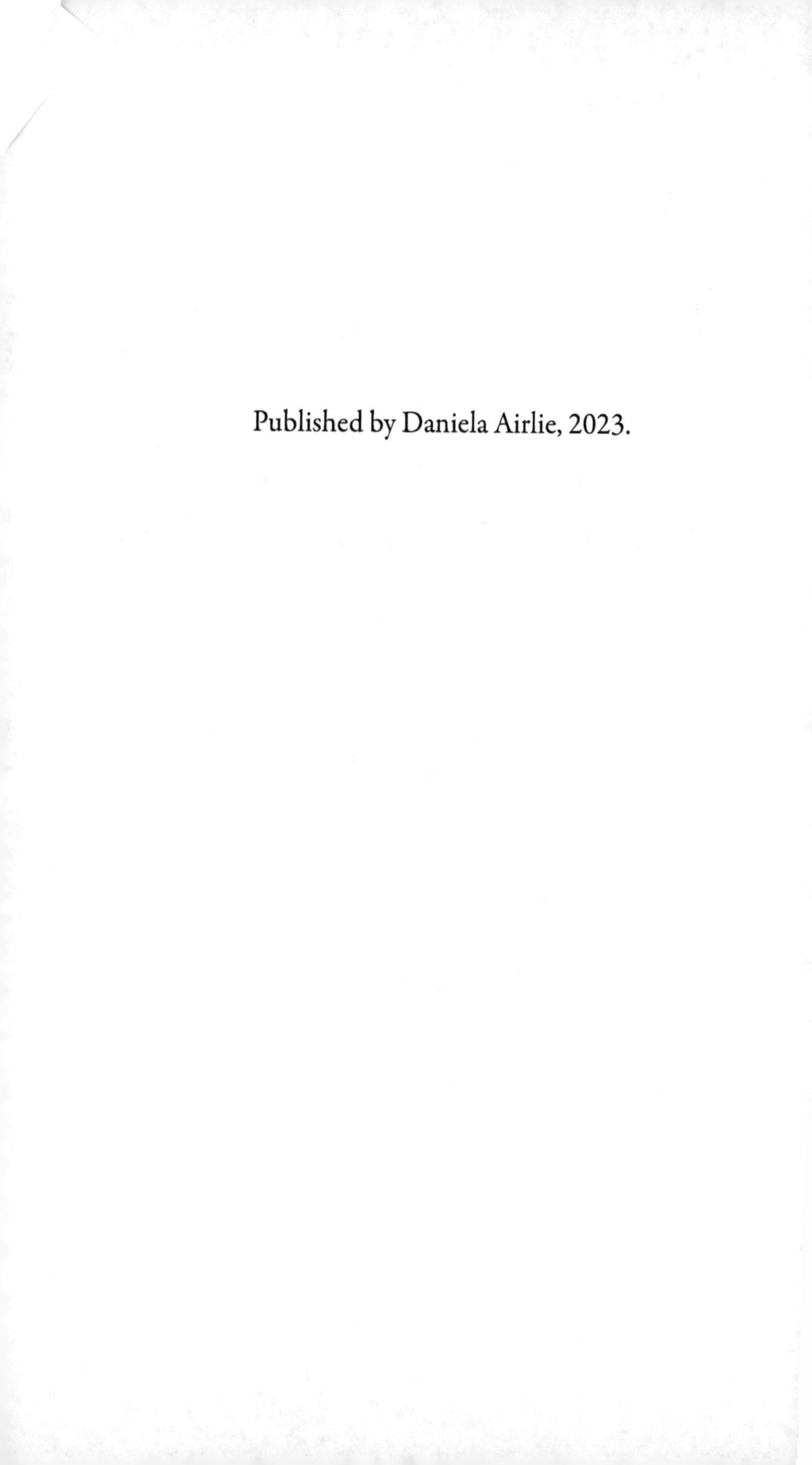
Published by Daniela Airlie, 2023.

While every precaution has been taken in the preparation of this book, the publisher assumes no responsibility for errors or omissions, or for damages resulting from the use of the information contained herein.

INFAMOUS CULTS: THE LIFE AND CRIMES OF CULT LEADERS AND THEIR FOLLOWERS

First edition. October 11, 2023.

ISBN: 979-8215603055

Written by Daniela Airlie.

Table of Contents

---

1. http://danielaairlie.carrd.co

Introduction

Cults are a fascinating subcategory of true crime, perhaps because their stories seem so unbelievable or too far-fetched to be true. From the outside looking in, it can be difficult to fathom how someone - no matter how charismatic or manipulative they may be - is able to collect a flock of loyal followers who will offer up their basic freedoms to join them.

Not only can these cult leaders seem to get hordes of people to believe their every word, but all too often, they abuse this power in the worst ways. Violence, depravity, sexual abuse, and death often ensue, making the very idea of cults (and their respective leaders) too intriguing to ignore.

So, what's so special about cult leaders that make people cast aside their comfortable existence to start a new, suppressed life where their actions and beliefs are restricted?

It's not always the fear of violence. Charles Manson was barely 5 foot 2 - hardly an overbearing presence. He was daunting nonetheless. It's always not money - some of the cults and the followers I'll detail in this book lived very primitive existences. It's not always the promise of a happy life, and it's not the allure of love and affection.

While all of the cult leaders in this publication are very different and unique from one another, most of them had one thing in common - their enigmatic charisma. This gave them a manipulative ability to lure in those who sought out belonging, no matter the price they had to pay for it. For all intents and purposes, cult leaders are people's people - until they're not.

If you're familiar with my books, you'll know I prefer to cover lesser-known crime cases. This theme remains in the *Infamous Crimes* series, where I'll detail six relatively unheard stories of cults and their leaders, documenting their lives and crimes, before ending this book by trying to answer the question: *why do people join cults*?

Roch Theriault: The Ant Hill Kids

The tale of Roch Thériault is as shocking as it is terrifying. Even if this case were a work of fiction - which sadly it's not - we'd probably deem it too farfetched to be a believable story.

Roch spearheaded a cult of individuals who he beat, tortured, and abused under the guise of being their prophet. Still, nobody felt able to stand up to the wicked man, enabling him to get away with some genuinely sickening crimes, many of which involved innocent children.

It's worth noting that much, or just about all, of Roch's violence was reserved for women, infants, and men much weaker than him. This case details these vile crimes, but before I cover the case of The Ant Hill Kids, let me tell you more about their leader.

Born in Québec in 1947, Roch Thériault's childhood bears no answers to why he'd grow up to be a power-driven, woman-despising killer. He was one of seven children of Hyacinthe and Pierrette and had a normal upbringing in the city of Thetford Mines. Roch was intelligent, a keen learner, and loved playing in the outdoors.

Although he'd later describe his father as physically abusive, this claim remains dubious. Not only because everyone around Roch at that time couldn't corroborate his story but also because Roch would later retract these claims. Still, during young adulthood, it seems Roch found that making outlandish claims and complaining brought him attention, something he basked in.

The more you delve into his upbringing, the more you see that Roch's childhood was run of the mill. In fact, it could have been described as "boring." He had routine, stability, and lived in an area where there was very little to do apart from making your own fun.

This boredom, coupled with Roch's need for people to give him attention, caused him to become what you may describe as a serial complainer.

At the age of 20, Roch wed his sweetheart, Francine Grenier, a young woman from a nearby town. After their nuptials, the newly married couple headed to Montréal, where marital monotony took hold. Francine got pregnant quickly, giving birth to Roch Jr, followed by little François.

Roch had been dealing with stomach ulcers for some time, and in the late 60s, he decided he had to seek medical help. He was told they'd need to be removed surgically, which was completed successfully. However, the aftermath of the operation took its toll on Roch. He was in extreme discomfort and struggled to digest his food properly. He took his frustrations out on his young family, his irritable stomach making him an easily irritated man.

After a few years in Montréal, Roch decided it was time for the family to return to Thetford Mines. A keen woodworker, Roch was using his skills to earn extra money. Still, the boredom of life in Thetford Mines and the indifference he felt toward married life saw Roch seek excitement elsewhere, namely in the form of booze and other women.

Under the guise of selling some of his wood sculptures, Roch would take off on weekends to Québec City to engage in extramarital affairs. Perhaps he did sell an item or two while on his travels, but for the most part, these trips were to meet women, something he found easy. Balding, big-bearded, and what you could describe as generic-looking, it was Roch's charm that drew women toward him, not his looks.

With him neglecting work in favor of women, it's no surprise that Roch's finances weren't in a good place. Eventually, he lost the family home, by which point Francine decided she'd had enough and left him. Roch made his way to another woman he'd been seeing, a young lady named Gisèle, and began a fully-fledged relationship with her.

Shortly thereafter, perhaps seeking more meaning from life, Roch stumbled upon the Seventh Day Adventist Church and decided to devote his time and energy to their message. He began reading the Old Testament and found he resonated with how masculinity was represented in the book. Roch took his new religious interest one step further by becoming borderline obsessed with the idea of the apocalypse. In particular, the idea of violent retribution fascinated him.

He also managed to make money from his newfound religion by selling bibles. With his natural charisma and passion for religion, Roch found this was a lucrative way to make money.

As well as his door-to-door sales day job, Roch also ran workshops for those battling addiction. These workshops proved to be a great way to recruit individuals to consider joining the Adventist Church.

In his work helping free people of their addictions, he quickly recruited a following of women. These women's backgrounds were different, but they all had similar traits. Not least of all, they were all vulnerable individuals seeking help for their addictions when they met Roch. They were all young. They all hung off Roch's every word.

The small brood consisted of Solange Boilard, Chantal Labrie, Francine Laflamme, Nicole Ruel, Josée Pelletier, Claude Ouellette, and a woman only named "Marise." Most of these young women were in their teens, the oldest being in her mid-20s. There were also two outlier males, Jacques Fiset, and another Jacques, Jacques Giguère and his wife Maryse Grenier. The only married couple of the group also had a young baby, which they would bring with them when they hung out with the rest of the crew.

It became more than a friendship for the youngsters who viewed Roch as a guiding light for them. The uneven power dynamic became even clearer when he encouraged his followers to drop out of college, which they did. After all, the world was coming to an end - what would be the point of a degree?

That way, they could spend their days in Gisèle's small apartment, lazing about on the sofa, helping themselves to food in the fridge, and overstaying their welcome in the woman's home. When Gisèle began her affair with a married Roch, it's unlikely she imagined things turning out like this. Not only was she having to share her apartment with his young friends, but it was clear many of these young women had feelings for Roch.

The only peace of mind Gisèle had that Roch wasn't involved with any of his young followers was that he'd been working toward becoming a priest. This meant he'd dropped lots of forbidden activities, drinking alcohol included. As we'll find out, Roch's beliefs and actions didn't always correlate.

Roch made a considerable effort to get his followers to believe he was chosen by God to "heal" people, something they readily believed. By 1977, he'd recruited two more young followers, Gabrielle Lavallée and Yolande Guinnebert, and conceived them to come live with him. With the group outgrowing Gisèle's apartment, Roch led his followers to the town of Sainte-Marie, where he set up an establishment called the "Healthy Living Clinic."

For all intents and purposes, the business looked legitimate. The girls all had their own uniform, a green tunic. Roch wore a robe but ensured his uniform was a different color to establish himself as head of the business. The company offered alternative medicine and would try and cure any ailment you may have, no matter how serious.

Roch was charismatic; there was no denying it. When you put vulnerable, sick people seeking help for their illnesses in front of him, he was able to convince them of just about anything. As a result, some of his clinic's clients joined his following, even moving in with him and the rest of the gang. Léo Faucher was one such client; he sold everything he had to join the commune.

Meanwhile, Gisèle felt as if she'd been put on the back burner. She felt her spouse had lost his once-obsessive love for her, and she was desperate to hold on to him. Not to mention, he had a plethora of young women clearly infatuated with him. At the end of 1977, Gisèle asked Roch to marry her. He didn't agree at first but eventually put the woman out of her anxious misery by saying yes a week after she proposed. By January 1978, they were man and wife.

It wasn't the romantic affair Gisèle dreamed of. Roch resumed his flirtation with the other members of the commune straight after the nuptials and refused to go on a honeymoon with his new wife. Gisèle thought the commitment of marriage would solidify her relationship with Roch - it didn't.

That spring, Geraldine Auclair visited the Healthy Living Clinic at the behest of her husband, who'd been drawn in by Roch and his promises of being a "healer." Geraldine wasn't suffering from backache or migraines - she had leukemia. In fact, she'd been getting hospital treatment for this, and the medication she was on seemed to be working. Her husband and Roch had different ideas. Roch took himself to Geraldine's hospital and got into a verbal confrontation with doctors about the medication she was on. Afterward, Roch convinced the husband to discharge his wife from hospital care and bring her to the commune. He promised he'd cure the sick woman.

This wasn't the healing retreat that was promised to the sick woman. She was cut off from her family and friends. She was stripped of the treatment that was keeping her comfortable. She was given grape juice as a cure for her cancer. It wasn't long before Geraldine Auclair died.

This clearly didn't align with Roch's claims of being an almighty healer. So, he told his followers he brought the woman back from the dead by kissing her, but decided it was "Geraldine's time" to be with God.

With his following growing, Roch decided it best to marry some of the commune off. Even if the man and woman he put together had no attraction or liking for the other, Roch's decision was final. In fact, he'd be the one marrying them.

Gisèle, understandably, was upset that her husband was doing this while neglecting his own marriage. She decided to stand up for herself and tell Roch that she was moving back home unless he abandoned the commune. Roch didn't take kindly to being given an ultimatum. His answer was a forceful fist to his wife's face before locking her in their room. He refused to let her out for 48 hours, during which Gisèle retracted her ultimatum. Perhaps the fact that she was pregnant with his child made her decide to choose the "safety" of abiding by Roch's desires.

By the summer of 1978, the Healthy Living Clinic shut its doors. It owed lots of money out and was causing more deaths than it had ever offered cures, so business wasn't as fruitful as it once was. The group had to move and, after bouncing from place to place, settled on the Gaspé Peninsula. Mountains and sprawling seashores surround this beautiful, remote area, perfect if you want to seclude yourself from the outside world. While here, Roch had an announcement to make: the anticipated end of the world was happening in less than a year.

In preparation for their imminent deaths, Roch told the group they had to live a righteous life and took them to a dry lake to set up camp and live out the rest of their days. He made the men of the group build a large cabin. This was an arduous task, considering they had few tools and amenities. They even managed to build a well. Roch, of course, couldn't partake in the manual labor since his stomach was playing up. Food was rationed by the leader, and should anyone complain of hunger, their food would be withheld. Ironically, most of the food was bought with the commune members' welfare checks. The group would combine their money at the end of the month, around $1400, and hand it over to Roch.

During this period, some members managed to escape. Yolande Guinnebert and Léo Faucher cut their losses and left. In Léo's case, he'd lost everything - he sold everything he had and put it into Roch's ill-fated clinic. Before the pair fled the commune, Roch warned them that God viewed them as evil for leaving.

By autumn, the communal cabin was finished. "Rooms" were partitioned by hanging fabric. Despite the lack of privacy, Roch managed to have extramarital affairs behind his wife's back. Eventually, one of the women went to Gisèle and told her she'd slept with Roch. As you can imagine, this caused great pain to the woman who went and confronted her husband. Again, he responded by attacking his wife, strangling her to the point she feared for her life.

Since Gisèle was now aware her husband wasn't faithful, Roch decided he wouldn't bother hiding this fact anymore. Quite the opposite - he denounced every marriage within the commune and declared *himself* married to all his female followers.

Another change Roch made was his sobriety. After a lengthy period of staying off his much-loved wine, he began drinking heavily again. He also began trading some of his followers to the local grocer in return for fresh food. Essentially, he was a drunken sex trafficker, but none of his following could see past his charisma.

Even when he beat the members of his group, they stood by his side. He'd only let them sleep when he decided they could. Should any of them dare nod off, the drunken leader would hit them about the head to wake them up violently. A young pregnant follower dared to eat too much at the breakfast table, causing Roch to fly into a rage over her indiscretion. He beat her up for her sin, breaking her ribs in the process.

Roch ruled with an iron fist and, even in his drunken stupors, was able to dole out severe beatings. You may be wondering, *why didn't anyone fight back*? There were more than enough of them to overpower and subdue the violent man. It seems as if none of the members wanted to fight back. It's as though they believed they deserved Roch's punishment and could not see how ludicrous and arbitrary it was. The group viewed him as a God.

Members would leave here and there, and anyone who managed to flee was branded the devil by Roch. The woman whom he beat for eating too much at breakfast endured one too many of Roch's outbursts and slowly started seeing sense. She verbalized her desire to move away from the commune, perhaps realizing her child wouldn't be safe if they grew up with someone like Roch overseeing them. As you can imagine, when Roch found out what the mother-to-be was considering, he wasn't going to let it slide.

Roch spoke with the woman's husband, a fellow commune member, and handed him an ax. "Cut off her toe - be a man, teach your woman a lesson!" he demanded of the terrified man. He put up some resistance against Roch's sick orders, but once the cult leader began questioning the man's sexuality, he took the ax to his wife's foot. He removed her little toe.

The fateful day when the world was supposed to end came and went. All the work the commune put into living purely and following their leaders' orders had seemingly been for nothing. Boulder-sized hailstones didn't come raining from the sky, flames didn't envelop the land, and everybody was still very much alive. Still, Roch had an explanation; mere mortals such as his followers didn't understand that God's time was different from theirs. The world's end was imminent, Roch insisted, and the group had to continue living as they were to secure redemption. This explanation worked - the group remained together.

Shortly after, Québec's daily newspaper ran a story on the group and their lifestyle but painted a different picture of how it really was for members. Roch was painted to be a gentle man who chose a peaceful life in the mountains. His followers were described as being free to leave at any time.

Despite closing the Healthy Living Clinic, Roch was still practicing alternate treatments and medicine for sick followers. Gabrielle Nadeau was undergoing some homeopathic treatments from Roch, but whatever he was giving her wasn't working - in fact, it sent her into a coma. Hospital treatment wasn't sought for the woman, who sadly died.

"Eternal Mountain" was the name given to the group's self-made home, and this was exactly where Roch wanted to bury Gabrielle, but the police got there before he was able to do so. They wanted to autopsy the woman to make sure the death was from natural causes.

With the cult leader taking his followers so far away from civilization, they weren't taking in as many new recruits as before. In fact, by the end of 1980, no new members had joined the group since they moved to Eternal Mountain.

However, Roch and his followers were on the local news from time to time, and this is how Guy Veer found out about the commune. Guy was depressed, so much so that he'd been hospitalized due to the symptoms of his depression. The man saw Roch on TV and was instantly drawn in and decided right then and there that he'd make his way to Eternal Mountain and join the group.

Once Guy made his way through the hills and found the commune, he wasn't exactly welcomed with open arms. He was permitted to stay but was segregated from the rest of the group. He wasn't allowed to sleep in the same place and was told he had to stay in a nearby shed. They'd feed him one meal a day, Roch agreed, but the man had to work for his keep. This included building cabins, collecting wood for the fire, and taking care of the children of the commune.

Not all the children - Roch didn't want the outsider taking care of his biological children. Instead, Guy was made to look after the children Roch considered "animals" - the babies he did not father. These were Samuel and Simon, both two and four-year-old Miriam. Guy did as he was told, and even though he was treated as a "lesser than" member of the group, he worked hard to retain his place there.

Guy was notably left out of the celebrations when there were parties or group drinking sessions. When Roch's two children from his first marriage came to join the commune, a big party was held to welcome the new members. Guy wasn't just not invited - he was made to babysit away from the joyous event.

It was clear that Guy was unstable, perhaps putting it mildly. Maybe this is why Roch didn't entrust the man with his own children - he didn't trust him not to do something cruel to them. Roch's gut feeling turned out to be right.

While everyone was enjoying the party, baby Samuel was crying loudly - this enraged Guy, who was trying to sleep. Eventually, to hush the child, Guy screamed in the baby's face that he best be quiet. As we know, yelling in a two-year-old's face for crying is as pointless as it is heartless. The child did not stop crying, and Guy decided to lift the baby up by his neck and punch him in the face five times. A truly barbaric, heinous crime that I can only imagine Roch saw coming - why else would he only allow the man to take care of babies that weren't his?

After the vile incident, Guy went to sleep.

The next day, the commune became aware that baby Samuel was limp, unable to hold his head up or respond to much at all. It was also noticed his penis was alarmingly swollen. There was no reason given for this, but what happened next defies comprehension. Roch decided to take a pair of scissors and pierce the child's genitals in order for him to urinate.

Gisèle would later paint a different story of that day, insisting there was nothing wrong with Samuel's genitals when he was found injured, and said Roch simply wanted to circumcise the boy. In order to anesthetize the toddler, Roch poured high-volume alcohol into his mouth.

Whichever way the event occurred, Samuel sadly died the next day from alcohol poisoning.

The baby's mother was informed of her child's death, and her reaction was stoic. She went back to her chores after being told Samuel had passed away. Later that day, the commune burnt the remains and scattered them.

Guy wasn't reprimanded or even scolded for his part in the twisted course of events - not right away, anyway. For months, things carried on as normal until Roch decided Guy had to pay for his crimes toward the toddler. This was pitched as the parents' chance at retribution - to make the person who attacked their baby pay for his sadistic, violent outburst. The mother and father of the child were given the opportunity, along with the rest of the commune, to decide Guy's fate. The outcome wasn't what you'd expect: the group found Guy Veer not guilty of a crime since they deemed him insane.

It seems this wasn't Roch's desired outcome, though, and after the verdict was confirmed, he decided Guy needed to be castrated. Guy was told of his fate, and although he wasn't best pleased, he didn't run for the hills. In fact, he willingly laid down on the "operating table" to be neutered. It did take a little persuasion from Roch, who told him he'd alleviate his persistent migraines by carrying out the operation.

The body parts to be removed were tied in an elastic band. They were hacked off by a razor blade and placed in a tissue to be thrown away. Guy spent the next week bleeding.

This wouldn't be the end of Guy's torment; he became Roch's very own punchbag. Roch would even tell the followers to stab Guy, which they did. Several at a time would run at the man and pierce him with blades until their leader called them off. It took a while, but Guy eventually decided he had to escape the commune. He ran as fast as he could to a nearby village. The police were called and made their way to Roch and his cult.

After finding some of Samuel's remains, the cult was arrested. A thorough search of Eternal Mountain took place, during which investigators found a letter written by Guy, consenting to having his testicles removed.

Criminal charges were brought to several members of the group after questioning. Along with Roch, Jacques Giguère, Maryse Grenier, Gabrielle Lavallée, and Guy Veer were all charged with harming baby Samuel. The parents of Simon were also charged with neglect. Roch and Gabrielle Lavallée were charged with the unlawful operation carried out on Guy. None of them accepted any guilt for their role in the crimes, though all of them were found guilty for their involvement in Samuel's death and Guy's fixing. Jail terms ranged from two years to just a few months, except for Guy, who wasn't deemed mentally competent.

Even jail couldn't keep the cult apart, though.

February 1984 came around, and the gang were all reunited. Roch had just been released and promised his followers that things would be new and improved.

He had sworn off alcohol again and promised not to use violence when reprimanding the group. They all followed him to their new home, Somerville Township, where they'd have to begin rebuilding their cabin from scratch again.

Roch had bigger ideas for his newest commune, though. Between the two men and nine women who remained part of the group, they built a home with a kitchen, a smokehouse, and a bakery. The group now had ten children, with four of the female members pregnant. Still, if the pregnant women were to "get out of line," Roch encouraged the two men to beat them into submission.

Money was hard to come by, particularly with so many mouths to feed. The cult members began heading into a nearby town to steal canned foods and luxuries like soda. It was only a matter of time before one of the followers got caught, and in the beginning of 1985, Jacques Giguère was caught taking items from a store without paying. This saw the entire group banned from the town center for life. With this obstacle in the way of obtaining food, Roch told his followers to get in touch with their family members and parents for help. Bear in mind that Roch had alienated his followers from their families prior to this and discouraged communication with those outside the commune. This rule went out of the window when he needed money, though.

As you can imagine, the family members were pleased to hear from loved ones but disappointed to hear they wouldn't be coming home. Some parents tried to bargain with their children, offering them the money they asked for, but only if they came home. This wasn't an option for the group, who were all heavily indoctrinated by Roch.

The next option Roch had was to use his followers to earn an honest living. It was a tough choice for workshy Roch, but one he had to make, or else the cult would starve. They began baking goods and selling them. As the members swirled around their bakery, cooking bread and pastries, Roch thought they looked like ants, working busily on their task at hand. This is where the name "Ant Hill Kids" came from.

Roch didn't partake in the honest work of making the goods. Now, money wasn't an issue, and the leader became bored. He tried to elevate this in cruel ways, one of which was making the women fight one another for his entertainment. The females would have to be naked, and there were no rules in these barbaric fights. Sometimes, Roch would set the women onto one of the men. He would also play mind games with each of the women, most of whom he'd impregnated at some point.

Roch also began drinking heavily again. His two promises - not to drink and refrain from violence - took mere months to break. If anything, the violence escalated. He would whip members of the group and hit them with weapons like his ax or hammer. While they cowered before him, he'd urinate on them. He would force his followers to engage in sex acts with one another despite their protests. One sick pleasure of Roch's was to smear feces on his ever-faithful followers.

Roch was doing all this for a purpose, he assured his commune; he was punishing them for their past sins. The end result would be a purified person ready to meet God when the world ends.

It was around this time another fatality took place. The death of Gabrielle's baby, although this time, it wasn't directly by Roch's hand. She took her son out into the freezing January weather, placed him in a wheelbarrow, and left him in the harsh weather for almost two hours. He died as a result. Gabrielle thought she was protecting her child by doing this since Roch - the father - regularly took his anger out on the five-month-old.

One of Roch's former "wives," who'd managed to flee the cult with two of her three children, had been acclimating to life outside of the commune. Roch would only permit her to leave if she left her eldest daughter there, a stipulation she agreed to. However, after having some time to digest the abuse and trauma she'd endured, she took legal action to get her child out of the cult. In doing so, she informed the police of what the children of the cult were put through at the hands of Roch.

This resulted in a more in-depth look into The Ant Hill Kids' children. They were malnourished, neglected, and even exhibited animalistic tendencies. Roch disallowed comfort and warmth toward the children. It was discovered Roch would pit the kids against one another, often encouraging stabbings and beatings. None of their basic needs were met - hygiene, nutritionally, or emotionally.

This was just scratching the surface. It was discovered Roch was sexually abusing the children, often making them do things against their will. Roch enlisted the help of his juvenile son, Roch Jr, to help him carry out the sexual assaults on the younger members of the commune. By the end of October 1987, the commune's children were made wards of the Crown.

However, Roch wouldn't be prosecuted for these crimes as there wasn't enough evidence to secure these criminal charges. Still, the children were all placed in foster care away from Roch's horrors and harmful ways. This didn't stop the cult leader from finding out where the children were and harassing their caregivers.

With no infants to use for his sick entertainment, Roch took out his twisted torment on one member he'd singled out: Claude Ouellette. He made the man tie an elastic band around his testicles and keep it tied all night. The man did as instructed and, in doing so, damaged his genitals beyond repair.

This gave Roch the opportunity to operate again, a task he was more than happy to do. It seems Roch had an unhealthy obsession with carrying out surgeries, though nobody could ever say he was a skilled surgeon. Quite the opposite, in fact. He performed yet another castration before asking the rest of the group if Claude should be killed. Thankfully, the members voted to let the man live, but that didn't stop Roch from using a gas-cutting torch to threaten the terrified man in front of everyone.

After this brutal ordeal, Claude waited for his chance to escape, fleeing into the nearby woods, where he stayed for a while. Instead of taking this chance to get away from Roch, he returned hours later.

It's hard to imagine, but the abuse would only escalate for Claude and every remaining cult member.

With a knife, he brutally attacked his wife, Gisèle, causing a huge gash in her thigh. This eventually became a clot, which was another perfect opportunity for the wannabe surgeon to operate. He pressed on the surrounding skin, bursting the wound wide open, blood gushing all over. He mutilated the area with a hot iron before finalizing the operation by pouring boiling water on the wound. Naturally, the wound became infected.

The sick man also began to use his acetylene torch to abuse the women in his following. He even used it on one woman as she was giving birth. He kicked his wife so hard in the ribs he broke them. He used a gun to instill fear into the group, shooting one female through the shoulder while doing so. He hacked at Claude's arm with broken glass. He convinced Claude he needed dental work and used pliers to pull the man's healthy teeth from his mouth.

Roch, in a word, was evil. Fueled by narcissism, a God complex, and a sick need for domination and violence, the man carried out a reign of terror on his followers - yet they all refused to turn their backs on him.

One incident even saw him create his own cocktail of unknown substances in a syringe and stabbed a female follower with it. He forced members to jump into the frozen-over pond near their living area. He would beat the pregnant women, breaking their bones without remorse causing miscarriages with great pleasure.

As 1988 was nearing a close, Roch was still heavily under the influence of booze most of the time. His favorite was cognac, but he'd take beer if he had to. In one of his drunken ramblings, of which there were many, he began stomping around the commune, grabbing the women's throats at will. "Your breath belongs to me," he warned them. In his drunken state, he chose one woman to carry out an operation on after deciding her liver was failing.

He opened up her right side and began removing tissue from the woman before sewing her up. After this, he placed her in a cold bath and then put her to bed. She died shortly after.

Afterward, in the only display of remorse exhibited by the cult leader, Roch began sobbing. However, it appears the guilty display was merely a show from the man. He even said he tried to drown himself but claimed a force - presumably God - pulled him from the water.

What he did next is truly sickening, even by Roch's standards. He got Claude to dig up the woman's freshly buried body and ordered him to drill a hole into her head. Roch then, in a disgusting display of evil psychopathy, carried out a sex act before the deceased woman. He ejaculated into the drilled-out hole in her skull. This was done under the guise of him believing it would resuscitate the woman.

When - to everyone's shock - the woman didn't return to life after the violation, the commune burnt her corpse, only after removing one of her ribs for Roch to keep.

Summer 1989 came around, and things remained much the same. Roch was eternally drunk, and the remaining members - Gisèle, Claude, Francine, and Marise - all managed to hide in the woods nearby until their beloved leader fell asleep.

Gabrielle elected to stay despite already being a victim of the violent dangers of being around Roch while he was intoxicated. He would again attack the young woman, stabbing her hand straight through so it was stuck on the table. She couldn't move - she didn't dare remove the knife from her hand or pull her hand free from the sharp blade.

Callous Roch left her stuck like this - pinned to the kitchen table - for about an hour alone. He came back, commenting on the woman's now-blue arm. He had a box cutter in hand and, without hesitation, began sawing away at Gabrielle's arm. Just below her shoulder, but before her elbow, Roch carved to the bone. The box cutter couldn't complete the full amputation Roch was apparently seeking, so he pulled the knife from his victim's hand and flung her mutilated arm onto a stump. He used a cleaver from the kitchen to amputate her arm.

You might be thinking that his reign of unimaginable terror *has* to be over now, that Gabrielle would surely flee and seek help from the police. However, Roch had more vile acts left in him, and young Gabrielle would bear the brunt of them.

A few days after the attack, he decided to operate on the victim's still-bloody stump. He used a pair of scissors. While doing so, he also took a chunk from her breast. The reason for this could reasonably be put down to pure sadism, not for any genuine medical reason.

Not content with this, he also used his ax to create a nasty wound on the side of her head. The head wound would remain untreated, and insects didn't take long to lay their eggs there. After another botched operation on Gabrielle's arm - this time using heated metal, which he kept dropping on her - the woman finally snapped out of the trance Roch had her in.

She waited until the coast was clear and made a run for it, getting herself to the hospital to seek proper treatment for her mutilated limb. She lied to the nurses out of fear of Roch's retribution, but they called the police right away. Authorities headed to The Ant Hill Kids commune and found the place desolate. Roch knew what was coming, and packed up the remaining crew and went to Québec. Only Roch and three members - Jacques Giguère, Chantal Labrie, and Nicole Ruel - remained from the cult's once-thriving member count. The remainder, thankfully, managed to find their way home after years of abuse from the man who promised to be their savior.

In October 1989, authorities caught up with Roch and his group.

Roch Thériault got ten years in jail for amputating Gabrielle's arm. Roch pleaded guilty to second-degree murder for the botched operation killing - but only did so under the bargain that no other charges would be brought his way. He was handed life in jail for this crime.

The sinister man fathered 26 children to a number of women during his time as leader of The Ant Hill Kids. Many of these children were thankfully taken from the commune and placed in care with families who offered the love and stability their father wouldn't.

On February 26, 2011, Roch was stabbed to death by a fellow inmate. He was 63. He remained unrepentant until his death.

Rod Ferrell: The Vampire Clan

A teenage vampire clan sounds more like an 80's horror film than a real-life true crime story. However, the tale of Rod Ferrell and the cult he founded, the Vampire Clan, is the true tale of a troubled teen and his descent into murder.

For the most part, cults are spearheaded by a charismatic leader, and the operations within are darkly sophisticated. This case is the antithesis of that. Although young and inexperienced, Rod still managed to run his own cult by claiming he was a centuries-old vampire. The culmination of his story ends in the deaths of two innocent lives.

Rod - or Roderick, but barely anybody called him that - was born in 1980 to his teenage mother, Sondra. The 16-year-old girl hadn't planned on getting pregnant. But, there was little else except mischief for the teenagers of Murray, Kentucky, to get up to in those days. Unless, of course, you left the small town in search of bigger things, which is what young Rod's father did shortly after his birth by joining the military. As a result, the young boy never got to know his father, but his young mother did the best she could with the little she had.

Still, there's no denying that being such a young mother would be difficult, particularly if the support network isn't rock solid. Baby Rod was frequently sent to stay with his grandparents since Sondra had to make a living. She would dance in clubs for cash, which eventually led to a life of sex work from her late teens onwards.

Rod would later claim his grandfather had begun sexually abusing him from around the age of five, but there was no arrest or charges brought to the man due to these claims.

Sondra could perhaps have been called immature. Who could blame her, after all, she was still a child when she gave birth to her son. But, even as she entered her 20s, her immaturity didn't seem to fade. She was interested in all things dark and macabre, which plenty of us are. However, she exposed her young child to these things from an early age. Bloody comics about vampires and gory horror films were things the child had access to and frequently indulged in. No doubt this had an impact on his teenage predilections.

The mother and son lived together in public housing, and life was okay for a while, although not abundant in money or luxuries. The pair only had one another, and the parent and child dynamic became skewed from time to time.

Still, by the time Rod got to high school, he found friends who weren't his mother. These kids had come from similar unstable backgrounds as Rod, and this could have been a great bonding factor for the group. The main members were Howard Anderson, Chasity Keesee, Dana Cooper, and Heather Windorf. The group were the outcasts, the social rejects who didn't fit in the mold their small town expected them to. They were into vampires, horror films, and moody clothing. This was the mid-90s in a small southeast state - to be different was to be avoided. That's what most people did for this group of teens - until they found one another.

The group decided to have their own hang-out spot, a rickety old building that had long been forgotten in the woods. They even gave it a name - The Vampire Hotel. All of this sounds like innocent teenage imagination until the rest of the macabre story unfolds.

At their self-titled hotel near Kentucky Lake, the youths did more than just tell campfire tales and make up curious vampire stories. They'd frequently buy psychedelic drugs and use them at their woodland retreat. They'd drink, smoke, and party in the forgotten building, bonding over their equally drab home lives. In between carrying out rituals and indulging in LSD, Rod and Heather wound up having heart-to-hearts, where she confided in him about her abusive father.

The abuse Heather described as "hell" included sexual assaults. This infuriated 16-year-old Rod, who would intently listen to his friend's sickening stories while imagining how he could save the teen from her abusive parents.

Heartbreak ensued for Rod when Heather announced the family was moving to Florida. The idea that Heather was trapped so far away with her father tormented Rod, who made sure to keep in touch with his friend after she moved. In fact, he ran up extortionate phone bills in his persistent calls to Heather.

In the end, the young girl's parents decided they'd had enough of Rod calling their new home and put a stop to it by banning Heather from using the phone. This devastated Rod, and he found it hard to deal with the fact that he could no longer speak to her. So much so he decided he would embark on a rescue mission.

He got the gang together and told them of his plans. They were going to save Heather, then flee to New Orleans and set up a new vampire house. Here, they could live as one big family, free of the judgment and oppression of Murray.

It is a simple, if misguided, plan at first glance. However, this plan didn't go as smoothly as intended.

The Vampire Clan made their way to Eustis, Florida, on a mild November day in 1996. The drive to Eustis would take 12 hours, breaks not included, but the clan didn't care; they just wanted to make sure their fellow member was safe. Not only that, but Rod had big plans for his young friend. He was going to "turn" her that morning. Heather had agreed she'd allow Rod to make her an immortal vampire, just like he was, by taking part in a ritual and drinking his blood.

The gang made it to Heather's parent's home, and the girl raced to the car filled with her only friends. The group was elated to be together again, excited at the prospect of moving to a new state and starting life afresh.

They didn't get far before the car broke down. Heather offered Rod her house keys so he could steal her parent's car, and they'd make their getaway to New Orleans. Before they did this, though, they headed to a cemetery to carry out Heather's "turning" ceremony.

The churchyard was empty apart from the group of teens, high on LSD, carrying out this ritual. Rod sliced his skin with a razor before encouraging Heather to drink the blood that poured. It was complete - Heather was now a vampire forever.

The gang headed back to the Windorf's to get the car. While the boys were getting the car, Charity and Dana took Heather to her boyfriend's place. This would be the last time she'd see him for a while, so she wanted to say goodbye before she embarked on her new life in New Orleans.

Meanwhile, Rod and Howard made their way to the Windorf's garage but soon discovered the homeowners were in the building. Heather's father, Richard, was fast asleep on the sofa in front of the TV. Rod and Howard decided to end the 49-year-old's life there and then. After all, Rod reasoned, he'd been abusing his daughter for years. *This was retribution*, he and Howard agreed. They'd managed to pick up a crowbar on their way to the living room, which they agreed would be used to bludgeon the man to death.

Rod stood over the sleeping man for a few moments before raining blow after blow onto his face with the steel weapon. Richard woke up mid-attack as the crowbar repeatedly cracked his face and skull. The man was knocked unconscious, his torso also taking repeated damage in the attack. After almost 25 blows to the head area, Richard succumbed to his injuries.

The violent attack wasn't anywhere near quiet, which alerted Heather's mother to the commotion in the living room. She was in the kitchen fixing a hot cup of coffee and carried it with her as she raced to see what was going on. She walked into a bloodbath. Her husband was lying in a pool of his own blood, his face beaten horrifically. Two teenage thugs in her living room stood over him. It was fight or flight for the woman, who instantly chose to fight. She lunged at her husband's killers, dousing them in the scolding coffee.

Rod initially decided he wasn't going to kill Naomi. It wasn't her he had a problem with, after all. But since she flung her steaming cup of coffee over him, that made up Rod's mind: she would have to die, too. He raised the bloody crowbar over his head and laid one violent crack onto the woman's face. The powerful blow was so ferocious it severed her brain stem. The woman died almost immediately. Still, that didn't stop Rod from raining blow after blow onto Naomi's face as she lay on the floor. He was full of rage, continuing his attack as her brains were visible to see on the carpet.

Before killing the woman, while mulling over how to diffuse the situation with Naomi, Rod had considered saying to the terrified woman, "I'd like to have coffee with you," as some kind of ice-breaker. Before he was able to say his crude remark, Naomi had given the teen coffee, whether he liked it or not, something that caused Rod to fly into a murderous rage.

Although the victims were dead, Rod and Howard weren't done with them yet. They burned the corpses, danced around the bodies, and burned the letter "V" into Richard's skin. Once they were done, they looted the house. The pair took anything they thought they could sell, like jewelry. They also picked up some credit cards before getting in the Windorf's car, ready to pick up Heather, Charity, and Dana to set off on their road trip. Upon collecting the rest of the group, neither boy told Heather what had really gone on in her parent's home.

Meanwhile, the lifeless, bloodied bodies of Richard and Naomi were left posed on their living room floor. Their faces caved in and their corpses mutilated, the couple were left for their 17-year-old daughter Jennifer to find. This discovery would be almost impossible to get over at any age, but finding your parents like this at 17 would have been life-altering for the teenager, a real, living nightmare for the girl.

The police were called, and a manhunt ensued.

Authorities weren't exactly hot on the tail of the gang, but with them all being young and relatively naive, police thought they'd slip up sooner or later. After four days on the run, the teenagers needed supplies: food, water, money for gas, and some cash to rent a motel for the night. Surprisingly, even the vampires in the group needed food to survive.

The five of them put their heads together and decided Charity would call her grandmother, who would send them some money for supplies. The request was agreed to - but Charity had no idea her grandmother was in cahoots with law enforcement. Not only had the call been traced, but Charity's grandmother had deceived her beloved granddaughter in order to get her home.

She told them to head to a nearby hotel chain, which they did. Shortly after, police swarmed the area and arrested the group of teens.

When faced with the heavy pile of evidence against him, Rod maintained his innocence. A rival vampire firm was framing him, he insisted. Of course, he could only carry on with this lie for so long - the evidence was clear for all to see. If he stood in court and proclaimed he was a 500-year-old vampire who was butting heads with other vampires, they'd laugh him straight to the electric chair. You might presume that Rod was, in fact, mentally unwell. He was troubled and drug-addled, for sure, but he knew he wasn't a centuries-old vampire, and he knew that murdering innocent people was wrong.

While awaiting trial, R0d was diagnosed with Asperger Syndrome, but to suggest this had anything to do with his bludgeoning two people to death would be insulting. In reality, it seems Rod was immature, possibly depressed, and dealing with possible Schizotypal personality disorder symptoms. Again, this isn't a reason for his double murder.

Howard admitted to being a party to the murders but was keen to stress he'd never laid a finger on Naomi. In fact, Howard suggested he'd tried to be the voice of reason for Rod, who'd flown into an impenetrable rage when killing the couple.

Howard's attempts at calming Rod had been in vain, and even when the victims were dead, the killer bent over them and continued to bash their heads with the weapon. His version of events was considered questionable, and it had been speculated that he was simply trying to minimize his involvement in the slayings. Howard received two life sentences in jail for his part in the bloody crime.

However, Howard's sentence was reduced in 2018 to 40 years behind bars, taking into consideration the 22 years he served. He will be released in 2032.

Charity and Dana got reduced sentences in exchange for a plea deal. Charity got ten years in jail, and Dana got 17. They are both free today.

Rod Ferrell was sentenced to death for killing Mr and Mrs. Windorf. In 2000, though, this was reduced to life behind bars due to a technicality. Since Rod was only 16 when he was apprehended, he just missed the death penalty, which has an age limit of 17.

The Windorf family was disappointed to hear of the reduction in sentences. They noted how Rod has never apologized or shown remorse for his crimes. Quite the contrary - at his trial, he stuck his tongue out and goaded reporters. The impact Rod and his vampire cult had on the Windorf's was immense, not least for Jennifer, who had to discover her parents in such a horrific way.

She said she was full of life and independent before that fateful November day. Rod and his crew robbed her of that, as well as stripping her parents of the rest of their lives. They were still young themselves, not even 50 years old, and had another lifetime of plans they never got a chance to carry out.

Little has been revealed about Heather or the impact this has had on her. You could imagine she felt, or perhaps still feels, a great deal of guilt for (however unwittingly) bringing such a twisted young man into her life.

Adolfo Constanzo: Matamoros Human Sacrifices

The foundations of any cult tend to be the same. They have a charismatic, manipulative leader. The leader will preach their extreme belief system and target individuals to join their cult. Once members are lured in, they're often isolated and manipulated, and violence and coercion are used to stop the members from leaving.

In fact, the more you look into cult follower behavior, the more you'll see that they don't want to leave, no matter how poorly they're treated. Cults come in various different forms, but the execution of their nefarious ways differs from cult to cult.

In the case of Adolfo Constanzo's cult, named *Los Narcosatanicos* by the press, he and his cohort carried out a spate of crimes we now know as the "Matamoros human sacrifices."

Adolfo Constanzo was born in November 1962 in Miami, Florida. His father was a Cuban immigrant who passed away when Adolfo was young. His mother then moved to Puerto Rico, where she met and married another man before the family moved back to Miami. Tragedy would strike again for young Adolfo when his stepfather died shortly after their move back to the States. He was only ten years old, but he'd suffered two prominent losses in his life.

His stepfather had left Adolfo a hefty sum of money, allowing Aurora to set up a comfortable life for herself and her son. The pair lived in Little Havana, the Cuban area of Miami, but they weren't exactly welcomed by their neighbors. The residents felt something was off about Aurora, a feeling they also bestowed upon young Adolfo. Call it a gut feeling, or perhaps the mother and son duo simply came across as strange, but their neighbors weren't wrong.

Aurora was heavily into cult rituals, voodoo, and occult practices. She didn't keep this interest to herself, either; she introduced these things to her son. When neighbors ignored Aurora or somehow upset her, she'd retaliate by leaving dead animals on their doorstep. As you can imagine, these twisted acts didn't help integrate the family into the Little Havana community at all. Still, this didn't cause any upset for Aurora, who was busy intermingling with others into voodoo and a religion called Palo Mayombe. This religion involved dark rituals involving human and animal remains and was shrouded in secrecy.

By 1976, aged just 14, Adolfo was encouraged to take on the practices of the religion and became involved with its occult style of worship. Meanwhile, he was also exploring his sexuality and spent a lot of time attending gay bars instead of attending school. He'd spend his free time during the day engaging in petty crimes like damaging property and stealing.

By the time Adolfo was 18, he headed to college but dropped out after one semester. Bad grades and lack of education didn't fluster the teen or his mother. In fact, they believed Adolfo had much bigger things in store. Aurora believed her son to be psychic, a trait that he seemingly proved to be true when he predicted the attempted assassination of President Ronald Reagan. This pleased the mother no end, believing his powers were going to carry her gifted son through life.

Sadly, though, Adolfo's power of foresight didn't help him out when he was arrested for theft in 1981. He had a few small interactions with the law but nothing as serious as he would later carry out.

The young man sought out a career in modeling, which took him to Mexico City. Adolfo's sexuality seemed to lean more towards men, so when he landed in the capital of Mexico, he explored this inclination further. To make money, he trawled the city streets with his tarot cards in hand, offering people a glimpse into their futures and possible fortunes.

The young man made a group of friends while on this work trip. Each of them represented a part of Adolfo's character. Martin Quintana admired Adolfo and blindly did whatever he asked. Jorge Montes was gay and also claimed to have psychic abilities. Omar Orea was obsessed with all things occult. Adolfo engaged in a sexual relationship with both Omar and Martin.

In the summer of 1984, Adolfo decided to make Mexico City his forever home and sought a new life for himself and his small group of loyal followers. He would set up a home with his two lovers, and the three of them would create a reputation for themselves as mysterious and magical sorcerers who were able to predict the future. This fame brought many customers to the trio's door, wanting their fortune told and their souls cleansed of enemy curses.

The fees for these services were not cheap; some of them were almost $5,000 a session. When you factor in the gang having over thirty regular clients, plus other random walk-ins, you come to realize their operation was hugely profitable.

When Adolfo first learned about the Palo Mayombe religion, he was introduced to an "occult godfather" who taught him many things about the practices he should follow - one of which was to take advantage of drug dealers. These people were non-believers anyway; *let them die from the drugs they peddle* was his philosophy. Young Adolfo paid heed to this teaching and implemented at scale it in New Mexico.

His way of making money revolved around taking advantage of people's naivety. As a leader of a small following, Adolfo was naturally charming and charismatic. He knew this and used it to smooth talk his way into gaining the local drug dealers' trust.

Once he'd wangled his way into the drug cartel's inner circle, he began offering them spells that would make these criminals invisible to law enforcement and ensure their safety from police shootouts. He offered street dealers a spell that would allegedly make them invisible to the police when they were carrying out a deal. These spells were eaten up by the smugglers and dealers, bringing in a pretty penny for the three "magical men."

One dealer with deep pockets even gave the group $40,000 for a package deal that would ensure Adolfo's services for the following three years. Naturally, the criminal expected a great deal in return for such a large sum of money. The magic "spells" placed over the dealer were clearly non-existent, but the trio needed to keep up the ruse. To retain this lavish customer, they needed to up their game. These men weren't the type you'd want to mess with - they carried guns in their jackets, were chauffeured around, and had men all over the city. It took a lot to impress them.

Instead of practicing rituals with their usual animal carcasses and bones, Adolfo decided to use human bones to awe his client.

By this point, Adolfo had amassed a number of disciples alongside the main three of Martin, Jorge, and Omar, and they were more than happy to do whatever their leader demanded of them. These followers weren't your usual cult devotees. Often, cult leaders seek out the vulnerable in society so they can bend and mold their subservient disciples to do as they wish. Many of Adolfo's followers were wealthy, well-to-do, socially admired individuals. In the ranks of his cult were physicians, realtors, and high-end models. In the mix were also nightclub performers and exotic dancers Adolfo had picked up while prowling the New Mexico streets at night.

Along with three of his loyal followers, Adolfo raided a nearby graveyard for human bones to loot. Naturally, this new, macabre practice impressed his gang of mob clients, and word spread about how Adolfo and his cult were working miracles for those in the drug dealing business. In particular, the Calzada crime family regularly used Adolfo's services to help them evade the clutches of the law.

Of course, the spells weren't working the magic for the criminals. As far as I can see, they created a placebo effect - it was simply luck affording the drug smugglers freedom from justice. Adolfo had also managed to recruit a gang of police officers into his cult, one of whom was in charge of narcotics investigations. More than likely, this was another reason the drug cartels were getting away with their crimes - not Adolfo's spells.

It's a fascinating idea that this cult leader could attract such unwavering loyalty from not only high-ranking professionals but also from organized criminals. His charm and persona changed to fit whoever he was trying to impress. After a few short years, Adolfo was intermingling police officials, sex workers, drug dealers, respected professionals, and low-ranking thugs. Together, they created a storm of corruption, spearheaded by their leader, Adolfo Constanzo. They all hung on his every word. To them, he was their God.

The money coming in on a monthly basis was more than many of us will earn over a number of years. Adolfo and his followers were able to drive around in expensive cars, enjoy luxury meals at swanky places, and live a life free from the shackles of money worries. The gang and their surplus of material items eventually outgrew their small apartment, so Adolfo bought a big condo in the heart of Mexico City for the group.

The thing about money is that it never seems to be enough. First, you strive for a million. But, you soon rearrange your life to accommodate all your newfound luxuries. Soon, that million doesn't seem as much. You start searching for even more money, and that's precisely what Adolfo did.

He began upping his sneaky, deceptive tactics to swindle extra cash. One instance saw him pose as an agent of the Drug Enforcement Agency and raid a cocaine deal taking place. He swiped the drugs being sold for himself and his cult to profit from.

Adolfo's cult and clients were violent, hardened, and often remorseless individuals. They loved the brutal shows he would put on when carrying out his "spells." To keep his customer base interested over time, Adolfo kept escalating the barbarity of his rituals. Eventually, that led to human sacrifice.

To think of human sacrifice being carried out as a magic spell is disturbing. To know that it was carried out as a show, as a form of entertainment for paying customers, is beyond sickening. The killings were elaborate, barbaric, and carried out in front of a baying crowd, there to catch a show as well as immunity from law enforcement.

Naturally, given Adolfo's roster of clients, the more brutal his ritualistic killings were, the more his customers trusted him. They weren't unfamiliar with killings in their line of work. The cult as a collective was a tight-knit group of criminals, and Adolfo felt like his criminal customers would do anything he asked. After all, his spells and rituals had kept them safe.

The cult leader decided he wanted to partner with the Calzada family and have a stake in their criminal empire. There was no doubt in Adolfo's mind that the syndicate would welcome him to their inner circle with open arms.

He was wrong.

The Calzadas had no interest in partnering with the witch. He was good at casting spells, but when it came to letting him become a partner, the answer was a curt "no." Business is business, and the family drew the line at doing business with the man who cast spells for them. Adolfo accepted the decline well; in front of the Calzada family, anyway. In reality, the cult leader was incensed. He had been rejected, something he wasn't used to and didn't take lightly.

He wanted revenge. Adolfo returned to his base and plotted how he was going to exact it. *How dare the Calzadas reject him?* He was the one solely responsible for their immunity from law enforcement. Naturally, Adolfo's revenge would involve murder.

On April 30, 1987, Guillermo Calzada, head of the Calzada family, went missing. Six members of his syndicate were also unaccounted for. When 24 hours passed, Guillermo's disappearance was reported to the police - ironically the same people they were paying to be "invisible" from.

When law enforcement searched the head of the family's office, they noted how there was a plethora of melted candles and items of a religious nature sprawled on the floor. This was concerning and resulted in a search of a nearby river. Officers didn't expect to find much, if anything, much less the mutilated bodies of the missing men.

The gangsters all had the macabre markings of having been tortured before their deaths. Some of their ears had been hacked off. Other victims had their fingers and toes chopped off. In some instances, their genitals had been mutilated prior to their gruesome end. Organs were missing from some of the bodies, including the brain and heart. In one especially barbaric discovery, one man's spine had been pulled from his body entirely.

The victim's blood, unbeknown to the police who discovered them, was used to fill Adolfo's cauldron for future spells.

Three months later, Adolfo met criminal empire brothers Elio and Ovidio Hernandez, with whom he would do business, replacing the income that came from the Calzada family. The cult leader would also meet the woman he'd proclaim to be his love - Sara Aldrete. The 22-year-old was originally from Mexico but moved to Texas for college. She met Adolfo via her drug-dealing boyfriend, Gilberto Sosa.

The fact Sara was in a relationship didn't do anything to stop Adolfo from pursuing a relationship with her. In fact, it probably provoked the man to chase the young woman even more. He flattered her, charmed her, and made her feel special. Her birthday was September 6, the same as Adolfo's beloved mother, a fact he used to convince Sara that they were meant to be.

The only thing in Adolfo's way was Gilberto Sosa. He vetoed that by making a call to the man to tip him off that his girlfriend was seeing another man behind his back - a dangerous cult leader named Adolfo Constanzo. The relationship was no more, leaving Sara to turn to her lover, who quickly made her "madrina" of his cult. He was the godfather, she was the godmother. The new female lead of the cult would easily settle into her role, taking part in sacrifices and carrying out acts of torture on the victims.

With the cult growing, the sacrifices became more elaborate and gory, and to evade police detection, the group moved to the desert just outside of Matamoros. They resided at Rancho Santa Elena, a desolate spot with nothing around for miles. It was perfect for carrying out sacrifices and disposing of the remains.

In the summer of 1988, they carried out a number of killings, including the murder of some crossdressers Adolfo knew, various drug dealers, and some low-level criminals. Adolfo only considered a sacrifice a success - or satisfying - if the victim screamed and pleaded for their lives. Should the victim refuse to play into Adolfo's torture and goading, by screaming and crying for their life, he'd be unhappy about the killing.

Ovidio Hernandez, Adolfo's new druglord client and friend, and his toddler son were kidnapped on August 12, 1988. The Hernandez family desperately turned to Adolfo, pleading for him to cast a spell that ensured Ovidio and his child's safety. The cult leader agreed and set his men out to acquire the victim that would become the sacrifice.

The cult assembled in the desert on a humid August night and put on a show with their terrified victim. The blood-filled evening was witnessed by the Hernandez's, and as expected, the following day, Ovidio and his son were set free. Naturally, the crime family felt sure this was because of Adolfo and his magical skills. He took full credit for their safety and found himself a trusted ally of the family.

Even the cult's followers weren't immune from Adolfo's sadism. His victim selection wasn't just reserved for strangers, strays, and low-level criminals. In the winter of 1988, loyal disciple Jorge Gomez fell into Adolfo's bad books by allegedly taking the drugs he ought to be selling. For his violation, Jorge found himself tied up in the middle of the desert, tortured, and his blood drained before being killed.

Meanwhile, the Hernandez family, in particular Ovidio, were getting closer to Adolfo and his cult. In fact, Ovidio admitted he wanted to be a full member of the group, and so an initiation ceremony was arranged at Rancho Santa Elena at the beginning of 1989. The ritual, which included the new member spilling blood, was carried out successfully. Afterward, Ovidio would be elated to find that his rival drug smuggler, Ezequiel Luna, was to be tortured to death as part of a ritualistic killing. This killed two birds with one stone for Ovidio; a competing criminal was taken out of the race, and he got to enjoy his rival screaming for his life.

The night was only made better when two more rivals entered the premises as the killing was underway. These men were subsequently tortured and killed in a similar, violent fashion.

Ovidio was having fun with his newfound status as a cult member and volunteered to help other members head out to the streets and stake out fresh meat. On a hunting trip that February, Ovidio suggested taking 14-year-old Jose Garcia as the sacrifice. Jose was Ovidio's cousin; this didn't stop the man from basking in the teenager's gruesome death.

In March 1989, Adolfo demanded a white man to sacrifice. He felt a tourist would offer plenty of begging, screaming, and pleading as their life was slowly and brutally ended.

The cult took to the streets of Matamoros in search of a man fitting their leader's description. They would find 21-year-old Mark Kilroy. He was abducted and slaughtered. Shortly after this, the cult murdered Gilberto Sosa, Adolfo's former love rival.

Little did the group of killers and drug dealers know their kidnapping and subsequent murder of Mark Kilroy wouldn't be forgotten or brushed off like all their other killings. Mark was a Texan student who was working toward a career in medicine. He found himself in Mexico to enjoy the nightlife and carefreeness before dedicating himself to his studies. Tragically, he'd never make it back home alive.

At the time, the Mexican authorities didn't care about missing drug dealers, sex workers, vagrants, or low-level criminals vanishing. They didn't put much, if any, resources into finding these missing people. However, Mark Kilroy was different. He had a family who loved him and demanded to know what had happened to him. Mark was reported missing, and even Texan politicians got involved in nudging the Mexican authorities to solve the case. This wasn't going to be a missing persons case that would be brushed under the carpet.

That spring, cult member Serafin Hernandez drove past police who were carrying out random car checks. He raced past their roadblock without a second thought - after all, Adolfo had placed an invisibility spell on him so that the police wouldn't see him. To Serafin's surprise, the police had indeed spotted him and jumped in their vehicles to chase the speeding man.

The chase took officers to Matamoros, with the suspect refusing to pull over the whole duration. When Serafin got out of the car, he goaded officers, daring them to shoot him. The bullets would merely bounce off him, he proclaimed, something Adolfo had promised him would happen if a shootout ever occurred. The police didn't take the man up on his offer, but they did detain him. The arrest led them to Rancho Santa Elena, where more disciples were arrested. It seems the police had inadvertently stumbled upon something more than just a drug smuggling operation.

Each member arrested would tell authorities similar things; that they indulged in black magic and human sacrifice. They told tales of torture and dismemberment with smiles on their faces. They did it for Adolfo and were proud to serve him.

A thorough search of the ranch took place, where they found fifteen badly tortured bodies. The cult members were telling the truth. But where was Adolfo Constanzo?

The chase was on, and for a while it seemed the leader had gone to ground. In fact, he'd made his way back to Mexico City with a small selection of disciples. His madrina, Sara, and a handful of followers were holed up in a tiny condo, unable to go outside for fear of being captured. Adolfo's magical powers seemed to be missing at the exact moment he needed them. Perhaps this fact made his girlfriend realize her murderous boyfriend didn't truly possess any powers at all. Maybe she already knew that and enjoyed the power and control being his love interest brought. Either way, by this point, Sara was done with Adolfo.

She couldn't tell him that, though. Her life would have ended if she dared to get up and leave. Instead, she found a pen and paper and wrote a note begging for someone to save her from the criminals holding her hostage on the fourth floor. She promised if she was rescued, she would talk.

Once she'd finished the note, she opened a window and flung it out, praying that it fell into the hands of someone who'd help. Sure enough, someone did find the note, and her pleas for help were indeed read. But the person who picked the note up didn't do anything with this information. Sara remained trapped in a small apartment with four violent men.

However, the four violent men found it hard to be four quiet men. They shouted, they argued, and neighbors even allegedly heard the noisy group fire bullets at one another. Eventually, the people beneath them called the police. When police arrived, Adolfo presumed they were there to arrest him for his murderous, satanic crimes. They weren't - they merely arrived to tell him to keep the noise down in the future. The cult leader's desire to remain out of jail led him to pull out his submachine gun and open fire.

What began as a routine callout for law enforcement turned out into carnage. Backup arrived, and the remaining cult members were cornered. Knowing it was all over, Adolfo threw his gun to El Duby, the cult's resident hitman holed up with him, and ordered him to shoot. Naturally, the cult member was hesitant to shoot his leader and refused. Adolfo warned his disciple that hell would await him after death if he didn't kill him and his lover Martin. This threat prompted El Duby to open fire, raining bullets into Adolfo and Martin.

The lovers collapsed into a heap on the floor, their blood seeping into one big puddle of crimson around them. With the threats disarmed, the police swarmed the apartment and arrested the remaining cult members. Numerous members over the course of the following months were also arrested on various charges ranging from murder to drug dealing to criminal association.

El Duby got 30 years in jail for murdering Adolfo and Martin. Adolfo's other male lover, Omar Orea, was charged with murder, too, but he lost his battle with AIDS before he was sentenced. The cult's godmother, Sara Aldrete, got a total of 66 years behind bars for her role in aiding and carrying out multiple murders. The cult killed so many people, many of whom had no friends or family to know they were missing, meaning it's almost impossible to put a number on how many victims there are.

Given the size of the cult and its deep connections within both higher-ups and the criminal underworld, it's also difficult to speculate how many members got away with their crimes.

Prior to his death, Omar Orea claimed that the cult was still very much alive and well. In fact, the cult that carried out human sacrifices was so renowned and revered that the remaining cultists have carried on with its teachings. According to Omar, the cult lived on and uprooted to the city of Monterrey. It's a terrifying - but not unbelievable - thought that this cult and its macabre beliefs still live on today.

Michael Ryan: The Yahweh Cult Of Nebraska

Little is known about Michael Ryan's childhood or life before he became a criminal. We do know that he managed to assemble a cult of impoverished farmers in rural Nebraska, setting up a home with the farmhands while preaching his religious beliefs. What he did after amassing his vulnerable following is sickening.

Michael Ryan was born in Nebraska in 1948. From the snippets of information available about his childhood, the boy had a normal upbringing. His mother was, perhaps at times, a bit too keen to discipline the child, but other than that, there are no stories of neglect or abuse. Certainly, there's nothing to help explain Michael's barbaric adult behavior.

Raised on a farm, young Michael would help out with the physical labor required to keep the farm up and running. He was an avid hunter from a young age, although he reportedly had an accident in his youth that saw him shoot his foot while out hunting. This allegedly caused the boy to lose some of his toes, resulting in a prolonged period away from school.

Michael was never academic in the first place, but the time away from his studies saw him get further and further behind his peers. Eventually, the boy dropped out of school and got work as a laborer. As he got older, he decided to take up truck driving to ease the burden his job put on his body. By this point, he'd wed a young woman named Ruth and had a young family to support, so the truck driving checks were certainly a welcome addition to the Ryan clan.

However, the damage to Matthew's body had already been done. His back was bad at the best of times, but hours upon hours spent on the road saw the man struggle. His back issues came to fruition when he was involved in an accident on the road, causing unbearable amounts of pain in the young man's spine. He even had to endure an operation to get him back on his feet, but after this, his days on the road were over.

Still, the pain persisted, and Michael took to smoking marijuana to help ease it. Without a job to occupy him and finances becoming a worry, Michael sought strength in religion and spirituality. His lack of a job, inability to provide financially, and boredom-filled days proved difficult for Michael to deal with.

His situation, one of pending poverty and his questioning of life's meaning, wasn't uncommon among the people of rural Nebraska. It was the early 80s, and the once-fruitful farming industry had taken a hit. The farming crisis saw many working families lose their homes and businesses and declare bankruptcy.

From poor weather conditions causing a great loss of crops to the banks lending farmers money they were unable to pay back to a fall in demand from buyers, the struggling industry affected many a farming family.

Just as Michael sought something to give him meaning again, so were many of the state's farmers.

Michael found solace in attending gatherings held by James Wickstrom - a white supremacist and far-right activist. His teachings were the opposite of Michael's childhood beliefs, but as he listened to James Wickstrom's talks, Michael began to believe in what the man was preaching. That Jewish people were the enemy, that homosexuals were asking to be killed, and that genocide was the only option for any race other than white. Michael attended more and more of these rallies and began to adhere to its tenets.

Despite Wickstrom's religion being based on Christian ideologies - with many of his own extreme ideas scattered throughout - many of the rules he preached actually stemmed from Hebrewism. This is ironic since Wickstrom was violently anti-Semitic, but nobody ever said cult leaders cared much about being a hypocrite. They referred to God as "Yahweh," which is Jewish. The foods Wickstrom promoted his followers to eat were kosher, again, a typically Jewish diet.

Wickstrom noticed Michael as being a regular at his rallies. Naturally, Michael made a beeline for the man, and the pair became friendly. Wickstrom taught Michael many things, one of which was a manipulative tactic he'd use many times over the years. It was called the "arm test."

The test consisted of holding an individual's arm and asking Yahweh a question. Yahweh's answer would channel through the person's arm. If Yahweh replied "yes" to the question, the person's arm would remain in the air. If the answer was "no" the arm would flop down. However, the person asking the questions had full control over the person's arm and would be able to manipulate their movements, thus being able to "answer" their question to God.

As juvenile as it sounds, this manipulative trick worked a treat for Wickstrom, and people truly believed in it.

It wouldn't be long before Michael got a name for himself as being Wickstrom's right-hand man. He'd ingrained himself in the religion - or rather, hate-filled beliefs - Wickstrom promoted. He'd finally found his meaning and his purpose in life. While attending a rally, Michael met a man called Rick, whose wife had passed away. Rick was left to bring up his three children alone as well as work on his dwindling pig farm. It was a struggle, and Michael saw the man's desperation. He invited Rick to move to his farm in Nebraska; they'd spend their days reading the bible, talking about their religion, smoking some weed, and collecting an armory of guns in preparation for their upcoming battle of Armageddon.

The "Armageddon" in question was a supposed race war, where white people would fight for supremacy.

This sounded like a good decision to Rick, who packed up his belongings and uprooted his small family to Michael's farm. His youngest child, Luke, was only five years old when the father made the decision to join Michael's band of followers, which was quickly gaining numbers. By the time Rick moved there, the farm had a number of followers already living there.

This was the beginning of the cult bowing to its leader's wishes, which only served to fluff Michael's ego. In fact, he began referring to himself as "The King."

The cult was growing slowly and steadily, amassing a following of 25 members who lived on-site at the farm. They'd all been taken in by Michael and his religious teachings. Most of his followers were farmers who'd fallen on hard times and needed a sense of purpose; many struggled for money and basic amenities. This vulnerability was something Michael utilized in luring them to join his cult.

None of the members had jobs, so they took to stealing as a way of making ends meet. They'd take cattle and thieve farm equipment to sell on, using the money to sustain themselves and buy more weapons for the upcoming Armageddon.

As with a lot of cult leaders, at some point or another, they tend to declare it's their right to have more than one wife. Their self-styled religion encourages that, after all. He also encouraged Rick to remarry and "gave" him one teenage cult member named Lisa to couple up with.

However, after some time, Michael decided he didn't want Rick to be with Lisa - *he* wanted to have the young woman as his wife. So, that's exactly what he did. His first wife, Ruth, felt powerless to stop this. As much as she didn't want to share her husband, she didn't feel like she could neither speak up nor leave him.

Around this time, Michael also began bullying Rick's youngest son, Luke. A man in his twenties, over 6 feet tall and weighing almost 240 pounds, felt it appropriate to physically harm and verbally abuse a five-year-old boy. However, the more you learn about Michael and his sadistic ways, the more you understand just how evil the man was.

Not only did Michael steal Rick's wife, but he was also pushing and hitting Rick's young boy for his own twisted pleasure. Rick stood by and accepted this, watching on as the cult leader beat his boy. Shortly after Michael had engaged in a relationship with Lisa, he found out she was pregnant. The timing of the pregnancy meant there was no way the baby was Michael's - it had to be Rick's child she was carrying. Of course, Rick would be punished for such an infraction.

As a result, Michael rounded up the followers, and along with his "Queen" Lisa - since he was the "King" - announced there were some troublemakers among them. Some of the followers didn't believe in their leader, the self-proclaimed "Archangel Michael." They were doubting his role as their ruler, and as such, would have to punish them. The three accused of being non-believers were Rick, little Luke, and a 25-year-old follower named James Thimm.

Notably, Luke had questioned the validity of the so-called "arm test," whereby Michael claimed he was channeling the answers of God through the arm. The five-year-old boy had more sense than all of the adults around him combined, and he was punished for calling Michael out on his lies. He, his father, and

James were banished to a farm trailer. From now on, Michael announced, the three would be classed as secondary citizens, slaves of the commune.

This was just the beginning of the sick and twisted punishment doled out on them. Vile Michael forced Rick to abuse Luke. Rick was also forced to rape James. Michael demanded that Rick do heinous things to his boy - things no child should know about, let alone have to endure - and Rick complied out of fear. The three weren't just subject to sexual abuse. They were also made to complete all of the work required to keep the farm running.

Michael continued his bullying of Luke, too. He'd spit on the child, beat him, and poured cigarette ash into the boy's mouth. One cold winter morning in 1985, Michael made his way to the "slave" trailer, forced Luke to get naked, and ordered him to go outside into the freezing cold snow. All the while, Michael - dressed in a warm coat, hat, and gloves - was taking pictures of the child in the subzero temperatures. In another instance, Michael entered the trailer and wrapped a bullwhip around the boy's neck to choke him with it.

Rick stood by idly. I have to ask myself, at what point do you put fear to one side and let your anger aid you in protecting your son? The reason Rick says he did nothing was out of fear of Michael. I find this unbelievably hard to comprehend; fatherly instincts ought to have caused the man to jump into protector mode. Instead, he loitered in the background as maniacal Michael tortured the boy. Even when Michael put the barrel of his gun in Luke's mouth - causing the five-year-old to wet himself - Rick did nothing.

In the end of March 1985, Michael's abuse of Luke would get too much for the boy's body to take. After slamming the child into a cabinet repeatedly, Luke was dealt a fatal blow to the head. Without guilt or sorrow, Michael ordered Rick and James to bury the boy on the farm in an unmarked spot - a horrifying end to a short life filled with tragedy and suffering.

Rick stayed in the cult for a few days after the murder of his son but eventually took off in the middle of the night. He didn't get help. He didn't speak to the police. He upped and left, leaving his two remaining sons at the Nebraska farm while he sought freedom.

This left just one victim remaining - James Thimm. He would endure beatings, torture sessions, and abuse on a daily basis. Around a month after Luke's murder, James was subjected to some of the most horrific torture a human has ever endured.

Michael and his followers, including his 16-year-old son Dennis and his close cohorts Timothy Haverkamp, James Haverkamp, and John Andreas, accused the man of poisoning their food. In retaliation, the four men and Michaels's teenage son took turns in raping the man. Each one of them did so to punish James for his alleged crime. The victim would endure severe internal injuries as a result. This wasn't enough to sate Michael's sick desires - he took the handle of a shovel and used this as a way to violate his victim.

After the prolonged sexual abuse, the men took turns using a bullwhip to brutally whip their victims. Each man doled out 15 lashings of the whip - that's 75 lashings for James. They first laid the man on his front, then turned him over to whip his front. Again, this bloody and vicious torture wasn't satisfying Michael's need to inflict unimaginable agony on his victim.

He decided to use a razor blade and a pair of pliers to further attack his incapacitated, but surprisingly still alive, victim. The sharp blade was used to skin James' leg, and the pliers were used to remove the flesh. The group of men then began stomping on James' mutilated leg, aiming to shatter it to pieces. They succeeded. The gang of men also took turns shooting James' fingers off.

Yahweh wanted this, Michael said. Michael also stated that Yahweh had indicated he wanted the victim dead by the end of the day.

Michael began pounding James' chest with his feet, stomping so hard he broke his ribs. He wanted to cave his chest in, he told his followers, as he violently trod on the victim. There was no way the man would make it out of the attack alive. Once he stopped breathing, and after shooting him in the head for good measure, the group of followers buried James in an unmarked grave.

You can't help but think, *what if Rick had gone to the police when he escaped*? It's likely James would have been saved. Sure, there was no bringing Luke back, but it would have ensured Michael was brought to justice before he could strike again.

Idle Rick remained just that even when he was away from the cult. In fact, the only time he went to the police was when law enforcement had already carried out a raid on the farm - two months after James' murder.

In June 1985, James Haverkamp and John Andreas were caught looting a farm for its machinery. This led to the police raiding the cult's farm, unaware that they were honing in on a religious cult with murderous members. Law enforcement thought they were capturing a crime ring dealing in stolen goods. The truth would be far, far worse.

The police immediately found a suspiciously large weapons cache, filled to the brim with guns, ammo, and dangerous melee weapons - much of it traceable as stolen. Naturally, this caused law enforcement to take a deeper look into the goings on at the farm, but they didn't need to do too much digging. Rick decided to come forward and offer up what he knew about the cult.

I understand fear. I understand how it causes inaction and causes you to freeze in moments when you ought to take action. But Rick's behavior - or lack of - during his time in and time away from the cult defies my comprehension. More so since his two other children were still at the farm for two months after he fled. The next murder victim could easily have been one of his own children.

Rick's story provoked another raid of the farm, which took place in August. The bodies of Luke and James were uncovered. Michael, Dennis, and Timothy Haverkamp were all charged with first-degree murder. The cult was quickly abandoned, and the main members were behind bars.

Timothy was eventually found guilty of second-degree murder. He served 23 years in jail and was released in 2009.

Michael and son Dennis' trial took place in March 1986. Teenage Dennis told the court he participated in the torture-murder because he felt it was what "Yahweh wanted." He was found guilty of second-degree murder, and his father of first-degree murder. As Dennis was handed life in jail, his father received a death sentence.

Dennis was freed in 1997 after serving just 12 years. He cut all contact with his father and regrets his actions, stating that his father had brainwashed him. He hasn't been in trouble with the law since and has held down a steady job as a truck driver since his release.

James Haverkamp and John Andreas each got 26 years in prison but didn't serve their full sentences. They were released in 1998.

Cancer caught up with Michael before the lethal injection could. In 2015, he died at age 66. His son, Dennis, upon hearing of the news, said, "Good riddance. Flush him down the toilet."

Larry Ray: The Campus Cult

If you went to college or university and lived in a dormitory, you likely remember it being a cramped, often messy space. If your parents knew the pigsty you were living in, they'd likely be appalled - pizza boxes strewn on the floor, out-of-date food lingering in the fridge, and unwashed clothes piling up in your room. For many of us, to even consider inciting our parents into our dorm would be too much to bear.

Not for Talia Ray; she not only invited her father to hang out in her dorm with her friends, she invited him to stay there. That's exactly what 50-year-old Larry Ray did when he made Sarah Lawrence College his home in 2010.

Sarah Lawrence College is a private arts college in Yonkers, New York. Surrounded by picturesque countryside and scenery, it's just a 35-minute train ride from the hustle and bustle of New York City. This made it an attractive place for artsy teens who are looking to make a career out of their creativity.

Prior to her father moving in with her, most of Talia's friends had already heard a lot about Larry. The student had made no secret of her admiration for her father and her disdain for her mother. Talia's parents had separated, and the 2004 divorce had been messy. Talia made no secret about her contempt towards her mother, who was initially granted custody of Talia and her siblings after the divorce. Instead of staying with her mother, though, the youngster chose to run away, and eventually, she lost contact with her siblings and mother.

More than this, Talia said, her father was a hero. He was the victim of a large-scale government conspiracy. Larry had exposed great political corruption, and because of this, the government was out to get him. In fact, that's why he was currently in jail, the girl told her friends. But, the loyal daughter supported her father no matter what, and days after his September 2010 release, she invited her dad to come live with her.

Talia lived in a two-story home with eight other students. Surprisingly, none of them flinched when their friend told them her father was coming to stay. They'd all heard so much about him already: how fantastic he was, how brave, and what an amazing man her father was.

Larry integrated himself with the houseful of teens quickly. He took on the role of "house Dad" - he'd cook dinner, arrange movie nights, and act as an agony uncle for those struggling. The 50-year-old didn't just make any old concoction for dinner, either. Larry's presence meant the houseful of kids didn't have to eat like your average student. He'd buy the best steak, accompany it with hearty side dishes, and finish it off with a tasty sauce, setting the table for the entire household to come to eat. When he didn't cook, Larry would order in for the house, making sure every student had enough to eat.

The dishes, the cleaning, and the household maintenance were seen to by Larry, too. It seemed everything Talia had been saying about her father was true - he really was fantastic.

Larry's dinnertime stories never failed to entertain his group of young, awe-stricken companions. He'd tell them tales of how he used to work as a CIA operative and recount mesmerizing stories of his time as a government agent. He stopped wars from happening and took bad people off the streets. He was in the Marines and was considered a big name among their ranks. The students lapped it up, believing every word to be true. How were they to know his military service consisted of 19 days in the Air Force in the early 80s?

He liked to talk, but just as much it seemed, he liked to listen. He'd offer his worldly wisdom to the youngsters around him, and they'd listen to his sage advice. He'd stay up late and talk to worried students about their concerns and struggles before retiring to his bed on the common room sofa.

Among the students who resided in the house were Daniel, Claudia, Santos, and Isabella. All of them came from differing backgrounds, but they all shared one thing in common: they were fragile, dealing with various degrees of depression. Daniel was struggling with his sexuality and didn't feel he had anywhere to turn. Santos had tried to kill himself prior to attending college. Isabella had just gotten out of a relationship and found herself lost in the world.

Each, in their own way, was battling inner turmoil. For someone as controlling and domineering as Larry Ray, this was perfect. He could worm his way in via their vulnerabilities and latch onto his prey for his own disturbing need for control.

Of course, these naive students didn't see Larry in this way, except for a few looking from the outside, like Talia's boyfriend. He noticed Larry spending more time with Isabella and his closeness to her becoming more blatant. In one instance, he saw the man lying on Talia's bed with Isabella, stroking her hair as she lay beside him. He promised the teen that no one would hurt her. Shortly after, Larry announced he was going to start sleeping in the same room as Isabella, *on the floor*, he stressed. Nobody asked Larry why he was doing this, but he offered an answer anyway: she was lost, and he was helping her.

Three months later, winter break rolled around, and the students were all packing up to make their way home for Christmas. Not Isabella, though. Larry had told her it wasn't in her best interests to go. The teenager had apparently confided in her older mentor that she'd suffered sexual abuse from a family friend, and Larry took this information straight to the girl's mother. He called Isabella's family just as she was due to be home for winter, stating the teen wasn't safe there and wouldn't be coming home.

These claims shocked the mother; Isabella had never told her she'd endured sexual abuse from anyone, let alone someone close to the family. "You let this happen," Larry spat down the phone to the confused parent. Instead of being with her family for Christmas, Isabella headed to New York City with Larry,

Talia, and Talia's boyfriend. The quartet stayed in an apartment that belonged to Larry's friend. The setup was bizarre - Talia and her partner were in the living room while Larry and his young companion stayed in the bedroom.

It was here, just a few months after integrating himself into their lives, that Larry really began exerting control. He told Talia's boyfriend he didn't need his anti-psychotic meds. He dictated when the group ate and what they ate. He ruled their sleeping patterns, managing when they slept and for how long. For Talia and Isabella, this wasn't concerning. However, Talia's boyfriend was ready to flee the situation. As soon as the group returned to Yonkers for the new term, he broke up with Talia and kept his distance.

This new level of control Larry was exerting spilled over into the student's house, too. He'd summon the housemates for "family dinners" and "meetings," which certainly didn't feel optional. He would lecture his young mentees, drilling into them that the universe is powered by their quest for potential, aka *Q4P*.

Q4P was, in fact, a philosophy of David Birnbaum, and Larry would teach this at movie nights and during family dinners. These lectures particularly interested Claudia, who had kept Larry at arm's length until the beginning of 2011. Q4P resonated with her, and she found herself drawn closer to the older man.

Claudia was known as being somewhat of an outsider, trying to fit in. She was known to tell little white lies to try and forge connections with her peers, such as saying she was a fan of a band she'd clearly never listened to. She also pretended to faint during one class to garner some attention.

Eventually, Claudia began seeing Larry privately. He was offering advice, direction, and showing concern for her well-being. Claudia, almost overnight, seemed to change. Once self-deprecating and giggly, the teen suddenly became obsessed with the Marines and their mental toughness. Her family knew something was up with Claudia but didn't know what. Claudia began telling her friends that she was dealing with schizophrenia. This wasn't just another misguided way for the teen to garner attention, though; she truly believed she was mentally unwell. It wasn't a medical professional who'd diagnosed her, though. It was Larry Ray.

Around the same time, fellow housemate Daniel was also going through a rough patch. He had a girlfriend but was sure he was gay. He had trouble digesting these feelings, and they brought him great anxiety. Naturally, he wasn't in a good place with his girlfriend and was close to breaking up with her. But, if he did, he'd have no place to live for the summer break. Daniel had a lot to think about and, for the most part, had shied away from going to Larry about his troubles. Daniel had seen him offer wild diagnoses to other housemates, such as Claudia's schizophrenia, and gave the man a wide berth. However, at Claudia and Santos' urging, Daniel gave Larry a chance. He arranged a meeting with Larry at a coffee shop and spilled his guts to the man.

"You're not gay, I can tell you that for sure," Larry smiled at his young mentee.

Of course, the young adult was acutely aware of his own sexuality. But Larry's words offered him some comfort and helped him feel as if he had direction. Not only that, Daniel felt validated by this straight-talking "tough guy" who was willing to hear his story.

Larry wasn't a dominating presence physically. He was average height, slightly overweight, and bald, but his presence was hard to ignore. He had an aurora, something that drew the directionless in and offered them hope. For Daniel, that's exactly what Larry gave him. Soon, the young man moved in with the rest of the crew and spent his summer in New York City with Talia, Claudia, Isabella, and Santos.

Life remained extravagant if super controlled for the young adults under Larry's watch. They were taken for fancy meals, handed cash from the older man's wad in his back pocket, and treated to designer goods.

On the flip side, their sleep was controlled. They were woken up early every day by the same rock song blasting through the stereo speakers. There were forced family meetings that would turn into hours-long lectures.

These lectures wound up becoming something much more sinister. They became interrogations, where one selected member of the group sat in the middle of the room and was interrogated by the rest of the group. Larry would take the lead, prodding the person to share deep, personal information about themselves. He'd mention childhood traumas and berate the person for how their damaged persona showed itself in their day-to-day living.

This would lead to Larry scolding the person for things they'd done to upset him, like smashing a plate or making loud noises while cooking. These were seen as accidents or mistakes by Larry, they were viewed as personal attacks. *They were intentional*, Larry would tell the person being interrogated, and it was all because of the childhood trauma they suffered.

These interrogations aimed to "break" the person being goaded. Only once they broke down would the interrogation stop. Once the group had achieved this "breakthrough," they'd applaud and cheer, making the interrogatee feel like they'd accomplished something.

These drawn-out nights would often spill into the early hours. Still, that didn't stop Larry from waking his group of progress up with loud rock music, despite the fact some of them worked in the mornings and needed their sleep.

Sleep wasn't something Larry was big on. He would use prescription amphetamines to keep him awake and alert, popping these pills whenever the urge to sleep struck.

Larry encouraged his young followers to write down their supposed transgressions and explain their behavior. One of Daniel's apparent misdeeds was playing the ukulele. *This was born from childhood trauma*, Larry insisted and made the student smash his instrument up. Eventually, Larry was able to convince his followers that they'd done things they hadn't, and these would be included in their written confessions of their wrongdoing. Complete control was exerted.

Around this time, Larry - who wasn't short of cash from his multiple income streams - began charging his followers for items they'd damaged. He'd accuse them of damaging his kitchen utensils or breaking his items and would bill them for it. In fact, he kept a list of the monies he was owed.

In 2011, Santos introduced Larry to his older sisters, Yalitza and Felicia. They would quickly join the ranks of Larry's followers. Felicia, in particular, caught Larry's eye. She was the oldest of the three siblings and had just begun a residency in Los Angeles when Larry began pursuing her relentlessly. He'd call the woman regularly, coercing her into his way of thinking. He wanted Felicia to be in New York with him. Eventually, he was able to convince her that, just like him, people were conspiring to get her. She couldn't ask the police for help, Larry insisted, because they were corrupt too. The only place she was safe was with Larry. So, Felicia gave up her residency program and flew to New York.

It wasn't long before Larry referred to Felicia as his wife, much like he already did with Isabella.

Meanwhile, Claudia was still very much under Larry's spell, too. Her parents had grown extremely concerned about their daughter's newfound persona. Suddenly, she was wanting to lose weight and go on strict diets. She became obsessed with the Marine mentality. Larry's words were seemingly coming out of her mouth. They also noticed their daughter began treating them with contempt for apparent infringements. For example, if dinner were late, Claudia would scold her parents for not being able to "run the house properly." These weren't her thoughts, the despairing parents agreed, they were Larry Ray's.

Claudia's mother and father were sick of the control their daughter's older housemate had over her. Not only that, but what was a 50-year-old man doing living among teenage students? They were confused as to how this had slipped past the dean at Sarah Lawrence. So, the couple arranged a meeting at the college and were swiftly told that the school was unable to stop any parent visiting their child. Larry's reign of control not only continued but worsened.

One night at the New York apartment, Larry decided to dive deeper into Daniel's sexual preferences. Unbeknownst to Daniel at the time, Larry had encouraged Isabella to begin kissing the teen. Daniel thought his housemate did so because she had a crush on him and, not wanting to face his sexuality, reciprocated the young woman's advances. Things ended up in the bedroom - at Larry's insistence - and the pair had sex. Larry remained in the room and watched.

This wasn't a one-off instance, either. Larry coaxed Isabella into regularly seducing Daniel so he could watch them. It was a game of control, power, and dominance. When this became boring for the older man, he began joining in on the tryst with the pair. Daniel didn't like it, and he began to think Isabella didn't either; she was just going along with it to please her mentor. These sexual encounters became more and more frequent, with Larry even inviting one of his friends over to join in on one occasion.

Summer drew to a close, and Daniel, along with Claudia, was due to move to England to continue their studies. Prior to her leaving, Claudia wrote an email to the Sarah Lawrence dean denouncing any bad things she'd previously said about Larry Ray. Initially, Claudia had expressed concerns that Larry was dangerous and manipulative.

While her gut instinct had been right, Larry eventually coerced her into his belief system. Claudia wanted to set the record straight that she didn't feel her mentor was any of these things. In fact, she admitted that she only said those things about Larry because his ex-wife had poisoned her into thinking this way. It's not clear how Larry's ex reached out to Claudia or why she would ever want to reach out to a random teenager to express her views about her ex-husband.

Despite being 3,500 miles from the campus cult leader, Daniel and Claudia couldn't escape his presence. Claudia certainly didn't want to be away from her mentor, and Daniel felt obliged to keep in touch with the man who'd "helped" him through dark times. While on a video call with the pair, Larry told the two they had to have sex. Larry knew Daniel was gay, and Claudia was reserved and shy. Still, the older man coached them through the act as he watched on. Even being an ocean apart from their leader didn't stop the domineering man from controlling them.

When Daniel and Claudia's year abroad ended, Claudia returned to campus while Daniel remained at the New York City apartment. Upon his return, though, Daniel found Larry had made some amendments to the place. Notably, he'd taken the handles off the bathroom doors, further preventing his young housemates from having any privacy.

Around this time, Daniel's parents, who'd noticed their boy drifting away from them, reached out to him to ask what was wrong. They sent an email, noting that their son was only aloof and unresponsive when he was around Larry. Unable to explain to his concerned parents what was really going on, the student began ghosting his mother and father. It was easier to cease contact than confront the truth of the situation.

Claudia's mother and father had similar concerns but were much more vocal about it with their daughter. In retaliation, Claudia arrived home one weekend with Larry in tow. Before the visit, Larry had told Claudia her mother must struggle to love her properly since she lost a daughter before giving birth to Claudia. This seemed to resonate with her, and she believed Larry's explanation as to why her mother was unable to dote on her daughter.

Larry brought up the loss of the child to Claudia's mother. Naturally, she was taken aback and argued that she loved her daughter more than anything and that the loss of her first daughter had no impact on the love she had for her second. Larry continued his poking and prodding of the mother, insisting she couldn't possibly love her child as much as she claimed. Eventually, the woman burst into tears. Larry's plan had worked - he'd broken the woman.

As her mother sat with tears streaming down her face, Claudia yelled at her that Larry was right - she *didn't* love her. Larry insisted he was on Claudia's team, and her parents were on another. With that said, and a wedge successfully put in place between the child and parents, Larry and his protegee left. At this point, Claudia's parents knew their child was under Larry's complete and unwavering control.

Daniel was still on Larry's radar, too. Talia messed up the application deadline for Stanford Law School, but Larry didn't blame her for the mix-up; he blamed Daniel for distracting his daughter. In fact, Larry argued, Daniel must have deliberately sabotaged Talia's chance at Stanford out of jealousy. Daniel denied these accusations, but nothing he could say changed Larry's mind. As punishment for the damage done, Larry was going to hurt Daniel.

The incensed man got some plastic wrap and some aluminum foil and fashioned a "necklace" out of them. The aluminum was rolled up into balls, and the wrap held them in place. Larry forced Daniel to remove his pants and tie the makeshift torture device around his genitals. Daniel, out of fear, complied. Larry intervened and tightened and twisted the contraption, causing the victim a great deal of pain. Circulation was stopped, and the foil balls made Daniel's skin bleed.

Shortly after this, Daniel again upset Larry by apparently damaging the oven. Whether he did or not, nobody would ever be able to prove it, but Larry was hell-bent on making the young man pay. He made Daniel get on his knees as he stood over him with a sharp knife, promising to dismember him.

Violence had been escalating for some time. Far from the genteel, kind "house dad" he presented himself as the year prior, Larry was now a brute who abused and hurt those who dared to disobey his teachings.

Santos also encountered Larry's cruel side. He began frequently choking the young man out, cutting off his airways from behind as the 20-year-old fell into a slumber. This practice is dangerous and could have easily resulted in Santos' death. Luckily, the man always came back around, but Larry remained cold and hostile toward his victim.

Daniel was becoming more and more ground down. Not only was he being controlled and coerced by his supposed mentor, he was having to suppress his sexuality. In a heart-to-heart with Larry, who was still insisting his mentee was heterosexual, Daniel dared to disagree. He claimed he was still having doubts about his sexuality. This caused Larry to fly into a rage. It's unclear if Larry was so intent on ensuring Daniel wasn't gay because he was homophobic or because he simply didn't want to be wrong about the young man's preferences.

Either way, Larry was going to teach him a lesson. "Isabella, go get a dress," he demanded. The woman did as her leader said, and while she was rummaging through her closet, Larry summoned the house to the main room.

"Put on the dress," he spat at Daniel. Too afraid to say no, Daniel put the dress on. Larry then made the humiliated man walk out into the hallway and lobby for others to see him. The rest of the house laughed at the spectacle while Daniel was dying inside. Once back in the apartment, Larry forced Daniel to carry out a sex act in front of the baying crowd. All the while, the young man was crying his eyes out.

After the sickening display, Larry took a devastated Daniel to one side to tell him that he'd humiliated him for his own good. This cemented in Daniel's mind that he had to get out, no matter what. In the spring of 2013, that's what he did when he moved to housing on the Sarah Lawrence College campus. Larry tried to reach out, but the traumatized young man refused any contact with both his abuser and his former housemates.

While Larry had lost one follower, he still had a tight grip on the rest. His tactic of claiming his protegees had stolen things from him or damaged his belongings ensured his followers were always in the position of owing him money. This caused a great deal of stress for members of the cult. In one instance, Santos even sent Larry an email itemizing all of the things he'd broken or damaged. These things included things that were just a few dollars, like masking tape, and items worth thousands, such as a cooker.

Santos had worked out he owed his leader $48,000. There was no argument from Larry about this. The panicked young man asked his parents for help. Naturally, his mother and father were dubious about these claims, and Santos' father even visited the New York apartment to verify all the damage supposedly done by Santos. However, Larry was there at the time and prevented the father from entering the property.

After meeting Larry, Santos' mother and father knew their son's acquaintance - or rather, his abuser - meant business. They rallied to get as much money together for their son as possible. This is just how much control Larry exerted over his victims. Just one encounter with Santos' father was enough to make the man crumble. The family even sold their house to give Larry money.

This eventually became Larry's main gig - blaming his followers for causing damage and then billing them for it. Toward the end of 2013, Larry took Claudia, Isabella, Yalitza, and Felicia to North Carolina to stay at his stepdad's rural home. Under the guise of a vacation, the trip was actually intended to put the followers to work. Larry forced his loyal band of young lovers and proteges to install a new drainage system, but in doing so, scolded them for damaging his stepfather's property. They all got a huge bill for the supposed damage.

Later that year, Yalitza ended up in a coma after taking a bottle of acetaminophen. Naturally, Larry took over, forbidding Yalitza from speaking to doctors or her parents alone. Yalitza was under the impression that Larry had saved her life by directing the medical team on how to treat her.

The following year, an eerily similar event took place. Claudia had taken a bottle of acetaminophen, too. She was rushed to hospital, and her parents were called. When they arrived, sure enough, Larry was at Claudia's bedside. She refused to speak to her parents. When Claudia's mother questioned the hospital why Larry Ray was beside their daughter, the nurse confided that she'd seen the man multiple times before in similar situations.

Isabella, too, tried to take her own life. While the students each had their issues to deal with, it seems too much of a coincidence that three of them tried to end their lives within three years of meeting Larry.

Claudia's parents struggled to deal with how their child was being controlled and dominated, and in 2013, they parted ways. Unbeknown to them, however, their daughter "owed" her leader a large sum of money for damage she caused to his property.

After graduating, Claudia struggled to find jobs that would pay her enough to pay off her debt. In the end, she turned to sex work, charging $8,000 a night. The money she made went straight to Larry. He knew how his protege earned this money and didn't discourage her from continuing. In fact, he congratulated her on doing whatever it took to pay her debts off.

By the middle of 2014, Larry was thrown out of the New York City apartment he was renting. His friend/landlord evicted him because of the damage to the property - door handles removed and renovations made - and the plethora of young girls residing there. Larry responded by suing his former landlord and brought Claudia, Isabella, and Yalitza as witnesses.

When Claudia took the stand, what she told the court was troubling. She was asked when she first met Larry.

She claimed to have known of the man since she was nine years old, listening to her grandfather talking about him and describing him as "trouble." She even suggested that her mother had sent her to Sarah Lawrence College in order to sabotage Larry Ray's reputation and cause harm to Talia. Claudia said her mother was paid to do this and actively encouraged Claudia to poison Larry. The troubled young woman even admitted to trying to poison the man before he won her over.

Yalitza's testimony mirrored Claudia's. Just like Claudia, she painted Larry as a protector, a guardian, and a compassionate leader. She claimed her suicide attempt was because she felt guilt over trying to poison Larry.

There was never any suggestion that either woman had ever tried to poison Larry - he'd simply been able to brainwash them that they had. The court didn't delve into the girls' disturbing testimonies in depth despite them clearly showing signs of indoctrination.

After the trial, Larry created a website dedicated to proving his young followers had been trying to kill him. He videoed Claudia's "confession." He ensured the camera caught him asking her if she was confessing of her own free will. "Yes," Claudia robotically replied before explaining how she had been trying to kill Larry and his daughter for the past four years. From putting mercury on toothbrushes to using arsenic, the woman insisted she'd never relented from trying to end Larry's life.

Up until 2018, Larry was cashing in on Claudia's profit from sex work. He'd had a hold over her for eight years, and as each year passed, the grip seemed to get tighter.

However, things culminated when Claudia reached out to a former employer for $500,000 to pay off her debts to Larry. This would be the catalyst for the young woman to find her freedom. By reaching out, the former employer began asking questions. Claudia confided that her mentor had been abusing her all these years. Some of the abuse saw Larry regularly tie Claudia to a chair, place a plastic bag over her head, and suffocate the young woman.

As you can imagine, Claudia's old employer was disturbed by the things she was saying, but there was no doubt she was telling the truth. Immediately, the good samaritan got Claudia far away from her abuser and ensured the woman moved quickly without packing clothes or any necessities. The most important thing was that Claudia got as far away from Larry as possible.

Claudia managed to get help to reverse some of the brainwashing and trauma Larry had caused, and her mother was elated to have her daughter back. Still, Larry had tried to reach out multiple times, even after Claudia changed numbers. He managed to acquire her new email address and sent her a lengthy letter about how he didn't understand why she was behaving this way.

Meanwhile, Daniel was also making strides in recovering from the abuse Larry had inflicted upon him. He'd managed to find the correlation between Larry Ray's behavior and that of a cult leader. It made sense to him now - a cult leader had indoctrinated him. This helped the young man on his path to healing, and he found a support group for cult survivors.

Larry was arrested in 2020 for the reign of abuse he carried out on the Sarah Lawrence campus students. Claudia had healed enough to find the strength to testify against him for forcing her into sex work while physically abusing her regularly.

"He destroyed my life," she told the court, adding that she had nightmares about the abuse he inflicted upon her.

Instead of being remorseful, Larry complained about prison conditions. He had not apologized or acknowledged any kind of wrongdoing for the abuse and reign of terror he carried out on the college students. In 2023, he was convicted of conspiracy, extortion, sex trafficking, and forced labor. He got 60 years in prison, meaning he will die behind bars.

Little is known about what happened to the remainder of Larry's followers. No doubt, even those who aided him in his nefarious activities were all victims of his coercion and manipulation. Hopefully, each of his former disciples has found peace and can see that their time with Larry Ray was nothing short of brainwashing.

Terri Hoffman: Conscious Development of Body, Mind and Soul

This cult leader never got convicted of any murder - but people around her dropped like flies in suspicious circumstances.

Born in March 1938, Terri Lee Hoffman had a rough start in life. She was born into extreme poverty and was placed in an orphanage just before she turned ten. While in the orphanage, the young girl allegedly had visions of Christ and was able to see the future through meditation. This may have become a coping mechanism to help the girl with the cold treatment she received. Young Terri believed her powers with all her heart, though, and used her abilities to discover she was the reincarnation of a saint.

She was eventually adopted by the Benson's, a couple from Texas who had lost their baby girl to tuberculosis. The couple gave young Terri something she'd never known in the 11 years she'd been alive - stability.

The girl didn't live with her new family for too long before embarking on a relationship with her older sweetheart, John Wilder. John was a dropout who drove trucks for a living, and he wasn't the type of man the Bensons wanted their daughter to end up with. Plus, Terri was barely 15 years old - she was too young for the so-called "thug" she was courting. The Bensons made it clear they didn't support their daughter's choice to date John. Defiant Terri and her older boyfriend headed to Oklahoma in May 1953 to get married.

It wasn't long before the couple welcomed a baby girl named Cathy. Baby Kenneth was born in 1958. Terri was just 20 years old and had the responsibility of two children under two to take care of. She took it in her stride, though, and began gardening as a therapeutic hobby. Another daughter, Virginia, joined the family in 1963.

Terri joined a local housewives group to alleviate the stresses of taking care of a young family. She found she was able to discuss her interests with these women - her meditation habit and her intrigue with metaphysics - something she was unable to do with her husband. Terri pondered big questions, such as the meaning of life and how the universe worked, but John had zero interest in humoring his wife and her interests.

Slowly, this interest led to Terri searching for materials that delved into the occult. John, perhaps trying to mend his and Terri's failing marriage, bought her a book on hypnotism. It was a purchase he would later regret - his wife became obsessed. She subsequently sought out positive thinking groups and people who were interested in all things mystic. In her search for a tribe, Terri slowly amassed a small circle of women just like her: housewives who were seeking to know more about the meaning of their existence.

Terri's charisma, enthusiasm, and likability saw people gravitate toward her. Soon enough, she was able to convince her small following that she was a messenger of God.

By 1970, Terri would hold meditation sessions that saw men and women alike bring their bath mats and scraps of material to sit on while they traveled into a hypnotic trance. Terri would guide her followers to a spiritual world where they would transport to the world's most sacred temples. She taught her students to travel to higher realms where their souls lived. From here, they could go anywhere they wanted.

She also claimed she could heal the sick. When her son, Kenneth, hurt his thumb in a nasty accident, pulling it from its socket, she used this as an example of her abilities. In front of her followers, she refused to take the boy to the doctor and chose to meditate until his thumb was fixed.

There were numerous dubious claims from Terri that were surprisingly believed. She made no secret that she was psychic and could see into the future. One day, she pulled one of her students aside and told him his girlfriend was going to die in a car crash. However, Terri could prevent this from happening - he just needed to meditate with her. The upset man and the "psychic" healer engaged in a lengthy meditation together, after which Terri congratulated the man - his girlfriend was safe from harm.

With Terri's sessions not cheap, money was rolling in for the Wilder family. She began selling her "lessons" - essentially the teachings of various religions curated into one new religion -

and accepting $100 a time for private consults. She would offer romantic advice to those who paid, and some of her followers would even give the woman money for no reason at all. One such person was Sandra Cleaver. She hung on Terri's every word and considered the woman her savior.

Terri's husband was getting increasingly concerned about how his wife was earning a living. He felt it was dishonest. When Sandy tried to give Terri a handful of expensive jewelry - bracelets and rings - John demanded that Sandy put her items back in her pocket. Sandy dropped to her knees and begged John to let Terri take the expensive gifts. This was the type of control Terri had over her diehard followers.

With her warm and comforting demeanor, Terri also attracted male followers who liked her in a more-than-platonic way. One such man always made a beeline to sit with Terri during sessions so he could be the one to hold her hand.

John's lack of enthusiasm for Terri's lifestyle caused the woman to file for divorce in late 1970. John got custody of the kids, the house, the furniture, and control over the family bank accounts. It wasn't long before Terri moved on - with the male follower who desperately had to sit next to her every meditation session. This was the same man she'd told her husband not to worry about, that her admirer was just a puppy dog following her around.

Terri and her new spouse, Glenn Cooley, went to New Mexico and got married, bringing fellow member Sandy Cleaver along for the event. Upon their return to Texas, Terri decided it was time to get serious about her following. She named her cult the Conscious Development of Body, Mind, and Soul, bought a new house, and began making a start on literature for her newfound group.

Things were looking promising for the mystic and her group. Terri's right-hand woman Sandy was essentially a cash-cow for the self-professed psychic; everything Terri told Sandy was believed by the woman. Some may see Sandy as gullible, but others may see the woman desperate to find meaning in her life.

Her husband, Chuck, didn't like Terri at all. He could see right through her, but Sandy wouldn't have it. "She can cure cancer," she told her unconvinced spouse. "She will put a protective shield around Susan," Sandy said, referring to her and Chuck's 13-year-old daughter.

Terri must have picked up on Chuck's dislike for her and began warning Sandy that her husband was negative and these vibrations were infecting her young daughter.

Sandy was behaving more strangely the more time she spent with Terri. She would profess she could turn wine back into grapes. She said she was a high priestess in her former life. Chuck stuck by his wife regardless, hoping her phase with Terri ended up being just that. However, it wasn't. When Terri claimed she was filing for divorce from Glenn, so did Sandy from Chuck. The reason she gave was that her husband was hindering her spiritual growth.

The divorce was messy, but Sandy got custody of Susan in the end. This was despite her questionable parenting. For example, she'd dropped Susan off at a neighbor's house before attending a session with Terri. The mother never returned for her child. She was clearly an unfit mother, but Chuck's lawyer advised him to accept visitation rights instead of full custody. The lawyer feared that if Chuck got custody, Sandy would retaliate by killing Susan.

Terri hadn't, in fact, filed for divorce as she claimed. In fact, Sandy paid for Terri and Glenn to take a trip to Hawaii - which, of course, Sandy had to join, too.

The Conscious Development of Body, Mind, and Soul made money from jewelry they made and sold. The items were made cheap and sold for extortionate rates, mainly because they were sold as having special energies. They often attended craft fairs to sell their goods, and Susan was always left home. She was looked after by Sandy's elderly nanny, Louise Watson.

The cult grew steadily over the years, and Terri had evolved the teachings to include the evil forces she called "black lords." The only way to fight off these evil spirits was by traveling to spiritual realms - luckily, Terri could guide people there to tackle these malignant forces.

Terri's relationship had been crumbling for some time, and Glenn began to feel discouraged with the lifestyle he and his wife were living. He left the cult in 1976 and filed for divorce. This didn't seem to faze Terri too much - she had her cult to focus on.

The Conscious Development sessions went from peaceful meditation groups to frantic, spiritual battles that the students were guided into fighting. After one of these hectic battles, it was announced to the group that Glenn Cooley had died.

His divorce from Terri had only been finalized just five days before his death, which was ruled a suicide. He was found unresponsive with deadly amounts of librium, a relaxant, and valium, an anti-anxiety medicine, in his system. He was 25-years-old. Glenn's will listed Terri as the sole beneficiary of his estate.

Terri never waited long between divorce and marriage, and just a few months after Glenn's passing, she married a man named Ben Johnson.

In August 1979, tragedy struck again when Terri's son, Kenneth Wilder, died after he fell from a building on a construction site. He was just 21 years old, but his assets were all left to his mother. Although his death was ruled an accident, there was no denying it was suspicious and brought more scrutiny to the death of Glenn Cooley.

Terri and Sandy's relationship also moved from strength to strength, with the latter becoming more and more enamored with her leader as the years passed. Sandy would take heed of everything Terri said, even when she made disparaging remarks about her teenage daughter. Terri had never liked Susan and told Sandy that the child harbored a lot of negative energy. This made the mother distance herself from her child, not wanting to become "infected" by her daughter's dark energy.

On a trip to Hawaii in 1979, Sandy and Susan got aboard an inflatable raft and floated out to sea in a mother-daughter excursion. This was a stark change from the mother Sandy had mostly been; she never took her child anywhere, did much with her, or bothered to interact with her much. In fact, at home, the teenager was forbidden from entering the living room - that area was reserved for her mother and Terri. She was relegated to her bedroom, only entering the living quarters when summoned to.

Susan wanted nothing more than to return home and live with her father. He wanted the same. For some reason, Sandy wouldn't let that happen despite pushing her daughter away at Terri's behest. The surprise raft trip took place just after Susan had turned 14 - coincidently, the same age she needed to be to choose which parent she wanted to live with.

While in the raft, a wave crashed into the mother and daughter and separated them, rendering Sandy unconscious. She awoke on the reef, bloodied and battered, unable to find her daughter. As Sandy was tended to, Susan's body was found hours later. Sandy's response was strange, although grief can do that to you; she suggested her daughter would be happier in heaven.

Susan - who'd, bear in mind, had just turned 14 before her trip with her mother - had seemingly written a will before her untimely passing. She left everything she had to Terri and the Conscious Development of Body, Mind, and Soul cult. But what would a child have to offer in their will?

Susan had a basketball, her record collection, and $125,000 in a trust fund that she really wanted her mother's mystic friend to have. It was reported that there was an attempt to cash in on the trust fund, which was eventually rejected and voided since children can't write wills.

It's been suggested - although never proven - that Sandy may have been the one to kill her daughter. Terri had always been in Sandy's ear about Susna's "negative energy" and "demons," something Sandy truly believed. Maybe Terri's words got to the mother, and she decided to take matters into her own hands by slaying the alleged demons within her child.

Shortly after this, Sandy took out a life insurance policy for a huge $300,000. She was just 40 years old, and the insurance agent reminded her of this, suggesting she go with half that amount. Sandy refused. She made Terri the beneficiary. Not only that, she transferred her leader the title to her house. Unashamedly, Terri would then charge Sandy rent to live in her own house. Still, Sandy bowed to Terri's every request, unable to see the woman for what she clearly was.

Louise Watson, Susan's former nanny and housekeeper for Sandy, had been a mainstay in the family's life. She was 77 years old, and her health was waning, so when Sandy suggested a trip to Colorado in September 1981, Louise initially declined. This wasn't like Louise - she'd normally do anything Sandy asked of her.

However, she felt unwell and unable to go. Sandy didn't take no for an answer and headed on the trip with the older woman, whether she liked it or not. They stopped off at Terri's sisters on the way before Sandy drove her car, with Louise beside her, off a 450-foot cliff. Both women died on impact.

In the months prior to her death, Louise had updated her will to leave everything she had to Terri. By now, the levels of suspicion toward Terri were sky-high.

In 1987, loyal follower Mary Alice Levinson's body was found in a Chicago hotel. She'd died of a drug overdose. She'd apparently injected herself with sleeping pills. Just a fortnight prior to her untimely death - Mary was just 33 years old - she'd put Terri as her beneficiary on her life insurance policy. Clearly, this cycle of people winding up dead after naming Terri as their sole beneficiary was more than just a macabre coincidence. But how could you prove it was anything other than this?

Towards the end of 1987, cult follower Robin Ostett committed suicide. In the lead-up to her death, she confided to her ex that she had viral hepatitis. Someone - apparently not a doctor - had told her she'd contracted the infection. However, post-mortem tests proved that she did not have the disease.

That same year, 39-year-old Charles Southern went missing, never to be seen again. He'd once been a follower of Terri and was heavily involved in the Conscious Development of Body, Mind, and Soul, but soon became disenchanted with Terri and lost interest in the cult teachings. Charles' vanishing is still unsolved, but many people believe Terri had something to do with it.

Terri's marriage to Ben Johnson had fizzled out, and she was quickly on to husband number four, 50-year-old Don Hoffman. However, in late 1988, he was found dead from a drug overdose. Prior to his death, Don had created a video of himself talking to the camera, somberly explaining how he had terminal cancer. The sad diagnosis came not from one but from three separate doctors. According to the man, the type of cancer he was up against was inoperable. It was a battle he simply couldn't win.

After the discovery of his body, the autopsy showed no signs of cancer. Terri would explain this by saying the black lords within Don's soul were "hiding" the cancer from the pathologist. As always, Terri was the only beneficiary of the deceased's estate.

Shortly after this, another body turned up, this time in a more grizzly fashion. Former cult member Jill Bounds was found dead at her home, brutally beaten to death. Jill had put a lot of time, energy, and money into Terri and the cult before leaving in 1982. Prior to her vacating the cult, she had been a loyal follower of Terri's. However, Jill was afraid of the cult leader, something that made police pinpoint Terri as a suspect. The killer had intricate knowledge of Jill's home - they knew her home security package didn't include the windows, so they broke in that way. Expensive items of Jill's had been stolen. The killer surely knew that Jill had some items of value in her property.

In the autumn of 1989, followers David and Glenda Goodman were found dead in an apparent double suicide. Their neighbor found them lying in their own blood at their home, two guns laid next to them. An entry in their joint diary marked October 20 as their day to "join their physical self with their spirit." Their bodies weren't found until weeks after their deaths. Terri denied having anything to do with the deaths, even stating she'd not spoken to the couple in months. The Goodmans' home was filled with Conscious Development of Body, Mind, and Soul, and in the weeks leading up to their deaths, they had written Terri checks amounting to $100,000. It seems Terri's insistence that she'd not spoken to the couple was a lie.

Still, Terri Lee Hoffman never did face justice for the deaths that seemed to follow her around. She did do some time in jail, but that was for bankruptcy fraud, and she was released after a year. She died at the age of 77 on October 31, 2015.

This cult case never saw justice for the bodies that piled up around the mystic leader. If Terri *was* telling the truth when she said she never physically killed anybody, her coercion, and manipulation did just as much harm in provoking her vulnerable followers to do her dirty work for her.

Why Do People Join Cults?

Why a person joins a cult is a difficult, although not impossible, question to answer. When I first pondered the answer to this, I immediately thought that the cult members who pledge allegiance to a leader are looking for meaning and are lonely.

But, then, not all cult followers were vulnerable and in search of someone to guide them - just look at Adolfo Constanzos' followers. To answer this question, I thought the best way to tackle it would be to ask, *what type of person would join a cult*?

Of course, being psychologically vulnerable is clearly a big factor in someone joining a cult. Those psychological vulnerabilities also help explain why such a person would stay in a cult even when it becomes abusive, suppressive, or begins to clearly show no regard for their well-being.

Look at Michael Ryan, who preyed on the farmers of Nebraska who were down on their luck. They sought meaning and a break from their bleak existence, and Michael, fueled by power and dominance, took them under his wing under the guise of offering hope. His desperate followers looked to their leader to guide the way and lead them to better days.

You may say that Adolfo Constanzos' followers weren't desperate or broke or in search of meaning. Many of his clients and followers weren't cash-strapped or lost in the world.

However, they did seek something from the supposed witch - immunity from law enforcement. Their vulnerability was their fear of incineration, something Adolfo took full advantage of.

The more you consider that many cult followers are vulnerable, the more you realize that this is mostly true. The first trait I believe a cult follower has is vulnerability.

The trait a lot of cult followers possess is that they were often segregated from society prior to their joining the cult. They were on the fringes of society, on the outside looking in, unable to "fit in." Those without a place in society are often welcomed into a cult by its charismatic leader, which ties in with the follower being vulnerable. They just want a sense of belonging, and a cult can seemingly offer that.

You'll notice a lot of followers have a sense of dissatisfaction with their lives prior to joining a cult. For them, life didn't work out how it was supposed to, and they attempted to regain some form of control by joining a cult. After all, cult leaders often promise change and amazing opportunities for would-be followers who are considering joining.

As we know, the promises of the cult and the reality of living in the cult are often very different. Violence, abuse, and control often ensue. Still, rarely does the cultist leave their new tribe, even after witnessing or even experiencing extreme abuse. Harm and danger present themselves to the followers, but they don't leave - why?

Cult leaders are more than just charismatic; they're manipulative, controlling, and adept at using coercive tactics to get people to do what they want. Followers are broken down via abuse but are made to stay through fear, guilt-tripping, and conniving tactics from the leader.

It's not as easy as the cult member running back home. Often, the follower may not have a home to return to - cult leaders often isolate their followers and stop them from having contact with their families. This enables the leader to have full control over their members without worrying about outside influence.

The threats a cult leader makes to their following are often heeded as the truth. "If you leave the cult, you're going to spend eternity in hell" is a toxic lie the followers believe to be true.

Steven Hassan is a mental health counselor with expertise in cult leaders' abilities to recruit followers and maintain their loyalty. It's called the "BITE Model."

BITE stands for behavior, information, thought, and emotional control.

Behavior control sees the leader dictate their follower's lives. They restrict their movements, diet, sleep, and finances. According to Hassan, the leader also exerts their control over the follower by using abuse, sexual assault, and beating to subdue their victim.

Information control is when the leader skews and withholds information from their disciples, like isolating them from family, lying to them, disallowing them access to the news or media, and planting certain information for their own gain.

Thought control sees the leader instilling a black-and-white way of thinking into the follower. *If you're not with the cult leader, then you must be against them.* This way of viewing the world allows for no gray areas. It encourages an us vs them mentality in the followers, which only aids in serving the cult leader's control over his disciples.

Emotional control is when the leader manipulates their followers into feeling guilty for their needs and wants. They make them feel like a traitor for being homesick or wanting comfort. The manipulative leader is also adept at making their followers believe that their own doing brings on any negative or unhappy emotions they have.

Digesting this information then begs another question: what makes a person decide they *want to be a cult leader*?

Narcissism is a big factor, as far as I can see. Narcissistic personality traits include a need for admiration, a desire for attention, a need for control, an inflated sense of self, and a distinct lack of empathy. I think that description also accurately fits one of a cult leader.

In a nutshell, I believe cult leaders are born from the person's innate desire to fuel their narcissistic persona. Not everyone with a narcissistic personality turns into a cult leader, but every cult leader has a narcissistic personality.

What do you think pushes a person toward joining a cult? What do you think pushes a person toward creating a cult? I think these big questions may provoke a debate depending on who you ask.

Thank you for reading *Infamous Cults*. I hope I've covered some cult cases that you'd not heard of before. My goal was to avoid rehashing the well-known cases and tell the tales of cult cases that were not front-page news or big stories. We all know of Charles Manson and his dark story, but there are cult leaders out there who were just - if not more - evil and deplorable than him. Knowing such evil existed - and still exists - in the world is a troubling thought.

I intend for the *Infamous Crimes* series to cover one true crime topic per book. This volume covered cults, the next will cover kidnappings, and I have plans to cover many other true crime subcategories within this series. I hope you've enjoyed reading this new collection (*Unbelievable Crimes* will still have regular releases, too) and that you look forward to more from this series.

If you would like to leave a review (which greatly helps me get this book out there), I would be incredibly appreciative. I am immensely grateful for my readers, and I'm thankful you took the time out of your day to read my content.

I look forward to seeing you in the next one!

Daniela

P.S. If you'd like to join my newsletter sign-up link, here it is: danielaairlie.carrd.co[1]

---

1. http://danielaairlie.carrd.co

Also by Daniela Airlie

Infamous Crimes
Infamous Cults: The Life and Crimes of Cult Leaders and
Their Followers

Unbelievable Crimes
Unbelievable Crimes Volume One: Macabre Yet Unknown
True Crime Stories
Unbelievable Crimes Volume Two: Macabre Yet Unknown
True Crime Stories
Unbelievable Crimes Volume Three: Macabre Yet Unknown
True Crime Stories
Unbelievable Crimes Volume Four
Unbelievable Crimes Volume Five
Unbelievable Crimes Volume Six